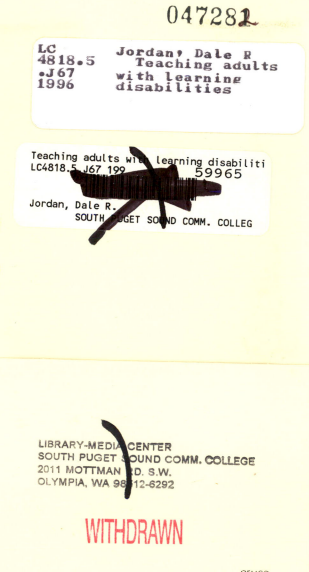

TEACHING ADULTS WITH LEARNING DISABILITIES

The Professional Practices in Adult Education and Human Resource Development Series explores issues and concerns of practitioners who work in the broad range of settings in adult and continuing education and human resource development.

The books are intended to provide information and strategies on how to make practice more effective for professionals and those they serve. They are written from a practical viewpoint and provide a forum for instructors, administrators, policy makers, counselors, trainers, managers, program and organizational developers, instructional designers, and other related professionals.

Editorial correspondence should be sent to the Editor-in-Chief:

Michael W. Galbraith
Florida Atlantic University
Department of Educational Leadership
College of Education
Boca Raton, FL 33431

TEACHING ADULTS WITH LEARNING DISABILITIES

Dale R. Jordan, Ph.D.
Associate Professor, Adult Education
University of Arkansas at Little Rock

KRIEGER PUBLISHING COMPANY
MALABAR, FLORIDA
1996

Original Edition 1996

Printed and Published by
KRIEGER PUBLISHING COMPANY
KRIEGER DRIVE
MALABAR, FLORIDA 32950

Printed in the United States of America.

Library of Congress Cataloging-In-Publication Data

Jordan, Dale R.
Teaching adults with learning disabilities / Dale R. Jordan.
p. cm. — (The professional practices in adult education and human resource development series)
Includes bibliographical references and index.
ISBN 0-89464-910-8 (alk. paper)
1. Learning disabled—Education—United States. I. Title.
II. Series.
LC4818.5.J67 1996
371.91—dc20 95-13766
CIP

10 9 8 7 6 5 4 3 2

To John, my beloved son and intimate friend,
whose quiet and courageous struggle to
compensate for LD inspired me to become
what I am today.

CONTENTS

PREFACE

I began my career of teaching struggling learners in 1957 before a definition of learning disability had been formulated. Those early years of classroom teaching in an economically deprived community immersed me in a sometimes violent world of struggle that was regarded as "lazy," "just won't try," "could do it but too stubborn to put out the effort." My ignorance of LD (learning disability) by whatever name it has been called compounded the pressures I placed on those struggling learners. Gradually it dawned on me that most of those nonreaders were bright when we worked orally. It was only when we turned to traditional literacy tasks that their frustrations boiled over into outbursts and rebellion.

The purpose of this book is to show how to reach out to the millions of subliterate adolescents and adults in our culture through strategies that successfully build basic literacy skills in LD learners. This is the first book to describe how specific differences in brain structure inhibit the mastery of reading, spelling, handwriting, phonics, and arithmetic. Never before have literacy providers had a manual that explains what causes specific learning differences, then describes successful strategies that enable LD learners to succeed in different ways. This book will be a rich source of information for undergraduate and graduate students who wish to learn about dyslexia, visual perception patterns that block reading ability, dysgraphia, dyscalculia, and attention deficit disorders related to classroom learning. The information in this book applies to struggling learners of all ages. Classroom instructors will find a wealth of practical information for daily lessons in working with LD learners.

Diagnosticians will learn how to identify forms of dyslexia, types of attention deficits, and visual patterns that interfere with reading. Tutors and literacy providers will learn how to adjust or modify traditional literacy expectations for LD learners. Program directors will see how accommodations must be provided for students who are LD. Counselors will have a wealth of information to help discouraged or depressed LD persons find new hope. Parents of LD children and mates of LD partners will find much information to comfort and encourage loved ones who struggle with literacy skills.

The chapters of this book come in pairs. For example, Chapter 2 explains the puzzling problem of "word blindness" that makes it impossible for persons with 20/20 visual acuity to see black print on white paper. Chapter 3 provides successful strategies that enable individuals to compensate for this devastating block in reading. Chapter 4 describes how genetic-based left brain differences cause visual dyslexia. Chapter 5 provides a wealth of strategies for accommodating for dyslexia. Chapter 6 explains the causes and characteristics of auditory dyslexia, while Chapter 7 offers a broad range of compensating strategies for this type of LD. Chapter 8 describes the causes and symptoms of dysgraphia and dyscalculia. Chapter 9 shows how instructors and LD learners can compensate for those forms of LD. Chapter 10 explores types of attention deficit disorders, while Chapter 11 presents successful ways to compensate for ADHD and ADD.

This book furnishes vital information for undergraduate teacher education courses. All new teachers will enter classrooms where one out of five learners will be LD. Teachers in training at all levels, from in-service workshops to graduate studies, will gain insight from this book that is not available in any other single source.

This book contains the heart of what I have learned during the past 37 years from my students, my research, and visits to countless LD adults in prison, mental hospitals, unemployment lines, the military, and the workforce. As study of the following pages will show, society faces a crisis of unbelievable proportions. The workplace is overwhelmed by an army of undereducated adults, many of whom have unrecognized and untreated LD. My prayer is that this book will bring relief and hope to those who struggle because of learning disabilities.

THE AUTHOR

Dale Jordan was born in 1931 in the middle of the dust bowl of the American southwest. His childhood education was in a one-room rural school where he experienced small group learning, peer tutoring, and an informal type of individualized instruction. His undergraduate degree was in English and philosophy at Oklahoma Baptist University. Following a European tour of duty in the U.S. Army, Jordan earned a master's degree in elementary education at Oklahoma State University. In 1957 he began several years of classroom teaching when there were no special programs for struggling learners. This hands-on experience with learning differences eventually led him to the University of Oklahoma where he earned a Ph.D. in educational psychology and reading education. During his doctoral studies, Jordan began researching LD patterns in prison populations, the military, and the workplace. He joined the editorial staff of the Economy Company to produce an acclaimed basal reading program. He spent several years as director of a university reading clinic where he developed field-based experiences for reading teachers with dyslexic learners. In 1973 Jordan established a private practice in diagnosing and treating learning disabilities. For 17 years the Jordan Diagnostic Center in Oklahoma City worked with struggling learners from around the world. In 1990 Jordan moved to Arkansas to be director of the Jones Learning Center at the University of the Ozarks. In 1993 he joined the graduate faculty in adult education at the University of Arkansas in Little Rock.

Throughout his career, Jordan has been a prolific author and workshop presenter. In 1972 he published the landmark study *Dyslexia in the Classroom* with Charles E. Merrill. He was co-developer of the *D'Nealian* writing program for Scott Foresman and Company. He has been featured in numerous film and video cassette training programs from Indiana University, Ohio State University, Marshall University, Kentucky Education Television, and Arkansas Educational Telecommunications Network. Through Modern Education Corporation and PRO-ED, Jordan has written a series of special education materials including *Overcoming Dyslexia in Children, Adolescents, and Adults* and *Attention Deficit Disorder: ADHD and ADD Syndromes*.

CHAPTER 1

What Is Known About LD In Adults

To establish the context for the information presented in this book, I must begin by telling a story that dramatically defined the focus of my career. In 1974 I delivered the keynote address for one of the first national conferences on learning disabilities in adults. As a young professional who had just entered private practice in diagnosing LD, I was on fire from daily experiences with struggling learners in prisons, in the workplace, in juvenile correction centers, in drug rehabilitation programs, in the military, with persons suffering from mental illness, with high school dropouts, and with youngsters who could not cope with classroom learning. My keynote address centered upon the need for traditional education to find new ways to reach millions of nonreaders and borderline readers being discovered in our society. In that keynote address I told stories of struggling learners I knew through my research and clinical practice. My address concluded with an impassioned appeal to literacy providers to find alternative ways to bring the riches of prose and poetry to those who cannot read literature for themselves. In 1974, adult literacy programs were still heavily grounded in traditional literary goals and values. "Not everyone in our society can read Shakespeare," I declared. "Nor should they. Adult education must develop alternative ways for struggling readers to discover the values of great literature when they cannot read great literature for themselves."

That presentation ended with two surprises that directly shaped my future. First, the several hundred conference participants rose in a standing ovation to demonstrate their own hunger for new approaches in adult education. Those colleagues were equally alarmed by the army of subliterate persons in our society. But the second surprise stopped me in my tracks. As I left the podium to the applause of the audience, my way was blocked by a furious person who backed me against the wall, shaking her angry finger in my face. I could not believe it. One of the most highly revered educators of the 20th century was contradicting my keynote address that had brought all those others to their feet in applause. "How dare you say that we must not teach Shakespeare!" thundered this diminutive pioneer with beautiful gray/white hair of her late seventies. "We must teach everyone to read and love the classics! How else shall we raise future generations to higher levels of fulfillment?" After more strong words protesting my upstart thinking, that little giant of remedial education marched away, leaving my thoughts in total confusion. That defining moment early in my career when two points of view collided like thunder clarified for me the dilemma that continues to challenge adult education. On the one hand, our society clearly needs to enrich the values and lives of all by sharing rich literary truth and values. Yet on the other hand, millions of youngsters and adults do not have the cognitive or perceptual ability to read literature for themselves. The following chapter will present new knowledge about learning differences and new ways to accommodate for those differences. Reasons why not everyone can hope to read Shakespeare for themselves will be examined. Alternative ways for nonreaders to enjoy the riches of learning in spite of being LD will also be discovered.

WHAT IS LITERACY?

Until the early 1970s, literacy was defined by rather narrow and highly traditional standards. To discover a person's literacy skills, teachers administered standardized reading and vocabulary tests. Those tests were normed for children and adolescents in classroom situations. Those tests required each person to read silently with no assistance. Each section of the test was rigidly timed. Most of the reading or vocabulary items presented multiple-choice responses. To save money, most schools and other agencies forced readers to mark answers on separate "bubble sheets" that were scored by machines. Literacy was defined by scores on such tests. Persons who scored above 8th-grade skill level were called "literate." Persons scoring below 8th-grade level were generally regarded as "illiterate." Before the mid-1970s, very little was known about learning disabilities or learning differences that distort an individual's ability to take standardized tests effectively.

In 1970 the first comprehensive survey was done of adult literacy in the American workforce (Harris, 1970). The United States Department of Labor reported that approximately 20 million adults in our workforce were "illiterate." That astonishing report stated that 20 million adults could not score above 8th-grade level on standardized reading achievement tests designed to test literacy skills in children and adolescents. This new knowledge of literacy deficits triggered great concern among national leaders. Congress soon funded the Right to Read program that sent instructors into the workplace to upgrade traditional reading and vocabulary skills of the adult population. During the 1970s and 1980s billions of dollars were invested in remedial literacy programs for older adolescents and adults.

At the same time this new interest in literacy skills permeated our culture, a largely invisible change was occurring in the definition of literacy. My 1974 keynote address theme to develop alternative ways to teach struggling learners was widely shared among adult educators. For example, Lloyd Korhonen innitiated major innovations in adult basic education in the upper midwest Region V (Korhonen, 1975). Through the Orton Dyslexia Society, Margaret Rawson proposed and demonstrated alternative teaching strategies for dyslexic learners (Rawson, 1988). Jonathon Kozol electrified public concern for the prevalence of illiteracy in the workplace (Kozol, 1985). Thomas Sticht stirred great interest in alternative learning for adults through his research with military units and workplace projects (Sticht, 1987). In 1983 the National Commission on Excellence in Education published an alarming study: *A Nation At Risk: The Imperative for Educational Reform* that underlined the urgent need for developing new concepts of literacy and remediation.

NEW DEFINITION OF LITERACY

By the mid-1980s a new paradigm of functional workplace literacy was replacing the traditional concept that literacy meant ability to score above 8th-grade level on standardized achievement tests (Kirsch et al., 1992c). Workplace literacy was no longer defined according to a person's knowledge of traditional literary standards. The new paradigm for adult literacy was based upon functional skills in three categories: (1) *Prose Comprehension Skills* (ability to understand basic printed information related to job performance or understanding current events); (2) *Document Literacy Skills* (ability to decipher tables, charts, and schedules related to job performance or getting along in society); and (3) *Quantitative Skills* (ability to do simple figuring in money management, filling in order forms, interpreting purchasing situations). This new model of functional workplace literacy did not replace traditional literary models that are related to formal education. Our culture still requires higher level literary skills for advanced education. However, workplace literacy is now defined by how well individuals can function in reading basic information, interpreting technical charts, graphs, and computer-generated information, and filling out a variety of forms and applications in order to be part of society.

This new paradigm of workplace literacy divides functional literacy into a series of levels of fluency. *Level One* places individuals at the bottom of the literacy scale. Persons who cannot or barely can perform without help in Prose Comprehension, Document Literacy, and Quantitative Skills are those who would score below 3rd-grade level on standardized literacy tests such as TABE (Test of Adult Basic Education) that is universally used in adult education. *Level Two* places individuals higher up on the literacy scale. These persons can do simple tasks in Prose Comprehension, Document Literacy, and Quantitative Skills. They would score at 4th- and 5th-grade levels on standardized literacy tests. *Level Three* places individuals still higher on the fluency level in Prose Comprehension, Document Literacy, and Quantitative Skills. These persons would score between 6th- and 8th-grade levels on standardized literacy tests. *Level Four* places individuals at the top of the functional literacy pyramid. These persons demonstrate high school and college level literacy skills on standardized tests of literacy.

NEW WORKPLACE LITERACY SKILLS FOR ADULTS

As this new model of workplace evolved during the 1980s, a major change was also occurring in literacy requirements within the workplace. As American industry has struggled to remain competitive in the world marketplace, enormous changes in workplace technology have taken place more rapidly than public education has realized. For example, Georgia-Pacific Corporation has become a leader in workplace education in order to sustain a supply of workers who can handle upgraded workplace requirements for Prose Comprehension, Document Literacy Skills, and Quantitative Skills. Georgia-Pacific Corporation selected the paper products complex in Crossett, Arkansas, as the site for its industrial Center for Excellence. By investing several million dollars each year for on-the-job skill training, Georgia-Pacific has addressed the issue of finding enough functionally literate workers to compete with world market labor conditions. In 1995 Gary Beasley, training manager of the job site Center for Excellence, issued this report:

> During the past 15 years, Georgia-Pacific has undergone an aggressive and extensive program of modernization incorporating the latest electronic and process technology in its production and maintenance sys-

> tems. This technology encompasses instrumentation and computerization using microelectronics, microprocessors, microcomputers, and robotics. Constantly upgrading management, production, and maintenance technology helps Georgia-Pacific and other industries compete in today's world market place.
>
> Job requirements for performing this high technology work has outpaced educational programs and in-plant training efforts. Entry requirements to the job market are much higher than what were required in 1980. . . . Traditionally, local industries have depended upon vo-tech schools and universities to develop a pool of potential employees with basic entry level knowledge for performing the type of work their employees are called upon to do. Due to changes in industry, higher education has not been able to keep pace in maintaining this pool of employees. (Beasley, 1995, pp. 2–3)

Irwin Kirsch, for many years a leading spokesperson for literacy needs within the workplace, has presented a sobering preview of workplace literacy requirements for the 21st century (Kirsch, 1992a). He foresees the workplace of the new century as a fast-paced arena of information processing. Workers will be required to do rapid comparing and contrasting of many types of data they see on paper, computer screens, and bar codes. Tomorrow's workers must rapidly integrate chunks of information that originate from all types of data bases, print sources, auditory records, and electronic networks. Workers must generate new information and develop new ideas based upon what they see, hear, and glean from many sources. Workers must be fluent enough in arithmetic operations to solve problems and interpret math-based situations without calling for help.

Like Georgia-Pacific, American workplaces of the next century will be high-tech job sites rather than the manual labor scenes of the past. It will be imperative for workers to have fluent skills in Prose Comprehension (quickly reading bulletins, E-mail memos, job descriptions, changes in daily schedules, safety bulletins). Workers must be fluent in Document Literacy, rapidly interpreting or producing computer-generated flow charts and graphic information. Workers must be proficient in Quantitative Skills as they rapidly respond to number information.

LOW WORKPLACE LITERACY SKILLS IN ADULTS

Within this context of rapid and profound change in workplace literacy expectations, adult educators are increasingly concerned by the implications of the most comprehensive study of workplace literacy ever done in the United States. In 1992 the U.S. Department of Labor released the results of an in-depth survey of workplace literacy according to the new paradigm described above: Prose Comprehension, Document Literacy, and Quantitative Skills (Kirsch, et al, 1992b). This survey was based upon current and future needs of American industry, as described by researchers like Beasley and Kirsch. The 1992 study of workplace literacy discovered that 45 percent of the current American workforce falls below Level Three on the workplace literacy scale reviewed earlier. Approximately 50 million Americans between age 16 and age 55 cannot function above 5th-grade level in traditional literacy terms. If Beasley, Kirsch, and others are correct in their descriptions of what our workplace will require in the new century, our society faces a crisis in workplace education.

This newly documented army of nonliterate American adults did not appear all of a sudden. Over a period of several decades, individuals dropped one by one through the cracks of the educational systems that did not know how to recognize or remediate their special needs and learning differences. Bringing these millions of low-skill adults back into classrooms, then into the workplace, can only be done one by one as teachers learn how to recognize learning deficits, then accommodate adult learning and workplace requirements to fit LD needs.

LD IN THE WORKFORCE

Within this vast population of semiliterate and illiterate adults are millions of bright individuals who have undiagnosed specific learning disabilities. Numerous leaders in adult education estimate that 8 out of 10 adults whose literacy skills rank below 3rd-grade level are LD (Jordan, 1988, 1989; Kidder, 1991; Payne, 1993; Pollan & Williams, 1992; Weisel, 1992). These literacy specialists estimate that some 30 million adults at the bottom of the American labor pool have specific learning disabilities that made it impossible for them to become literate during their years in formal education. As adults, residual LD patterns continue to block their ability to meet workplace demands for independent reading, writing, spelling, and arithmetic. These lifelong struggling learners cannot find employment that pays a living wage. They cannot fill out job application forms or apply for assistance unless they have help. They are often helpless and isolated in a culture that places increasing pressures upon workers to read, spell, and interpret information at high school levels (Kirsch et al., 1992). Yet they are intelligent, talented persons with a great deal to contribute to society. As later chapters will show, these frustrated citizens have carried unrecognized and untreated LD stumbling blocks out of childhood, through adolescence, and into adulthood.

WHAT IS LEARNING DISABILITY?

For almost 200 years scholars and scientists have tried to define disabilities that block language processing and school learning. In 1809 the German neurologist Franz-Joseph Gall was the first to describe the functional structure of the central nervous system (Gall & Spurzheim, 1809). This new knowledge of brain structure paved the way for the pioneering work of Pierre Paul Broca (1861) who documented changes in brain structure related to loss of speech (cited by Opp, 1994). Following Broca's lead, the English neurologist Henry Charlton Bastian (1869) coined the term *agraphia* to describe written language deficits among aphasic patients (Bastian, 1869). At the same time, a German neurologist Theodor Meynert (1868) was the first to show that certain psychological functions are associated with specific regions of the brain (Meynert, 1868). A few years later a fellow German physician, Carl Wernicke, developed the first map of how the left brain produces speech (Wernicke, 1874). Also in 1874 John Hughlings Jackson developed the concept that the left brain controls most of the language processing involved in oral communication. In 1885 Ludwig Lichtheim documented seven types of speech disturbance related to interruptions of specific nerve pathways in the left brain. He coined the term *alexia* to describe disturbances in reading. Lichtheim was the first to associate handwriting with the ability to read printed symbols (Lichtheim, 1885). Also in 1885 Hubert Grashey published his studies of the relationships between certain types of skull fractures to loss of language, memory, and perception (Grashey, 1885). Meanwhile, the German ophthalmologist Reinhold Berlin (1884) introduced the term *dyslexia* to describe poor reading ability in students who had good vision (Berlin, 1884). In 1872 Sir William Broadbent introduced the term *word blindness* to the growing research into dyslexia.

By the late 1800s other European physicians and educators were exploring the dilemma of why bright learners could not master basic literacy skills regardless of how they were taught. During the 1880s a Scottish eye surgeon, James Hinshelwood, began to diagnose a specific type of reading dysfunction that prevented the reader from recognizing what was seen on the printed page. Hinshelwood adopted Berlin's term word blindness to describe this perceptual deficit in reading (Hinshelwood, 1900). Using this newly developed model, a British educator James Kerr began a series of studies to identify word blind students within the British educational system (cited in Jordan, 1989). In 1892 J. K. Goldscheider developed the concept that reading requires integration of brain regions that process sounds, interpret spatial relationships, and comprehend time sequence (Goldscheider, 1892).

In the early 1920s Samuel T. Orton, a neuropathologist, became intrigued by language disabilities he discovered in soldiers who had sustained head injuries during World War I. Orton coined the term *strephosymbolia* to describe the "twisted symbol" patterns he found when certain types of left brain injuries had occurred. In 1925 Orton linked Hinshelwood's work with word blindness to types of reading disabilities he found in brain-injured adults (Orton, 1925). In 1937 Orton wrote that dyslexia is a dysfunction in visual perception and visual memory caused by deficits in brain structure (Orton, 1937). During the 1930s the term *specific language disability (SLD)* became widely used to designate major struggle with reading, language usage, and spelling.

In the early 1940s Stanley Taylor became interested in poor eye teaming patterns he was seeing in struggling readers. For two decades he documented irregular saccadic (eye movement) patterns in SLD students by photographing their vision patterns while they read (Taylor, 1960). In 1962 Samuel Kirk introduced the concept of *learning disability* (LD) that rapidly became the hallmark designation for those who struggle to learn (cited in Hammill, 1990). In 1963 Samuel Clements introduced the concept *minimal brain dysfunction* (MBD) to describe struggling learners who could not pay attention, were overly irritable in formal learning, could not absorb new information on schedule, and could not thrive in mainstream classrooms (Clements, 1966). In 1972 Jordan published the landmark study *Dyslexia in the Classroom* that documented the ways in which dyslexia blocks classroom learning for many bright students of all ages (Jordan, 1972). A common theme ran through all of these historical efforts to describe and define barriers to learning. Researchers agreed that LD, however it is defined, begins with good intelligence. To be LD, one is assumed to have average or above average intelligence (Hammill, 1990; Jordan, 1988, 1989, 1992b; Rawson, 1988; Weisel, 1992).

Defining Learning Disability

For more than 100 years researchers and educators have tried to develop a universally accepted definition of learning disability. By the early 1980s more than 200 definitions of LD could be found in professional literature (Evans, 1982). By 1990 the umbrella label LD represented four different but overlapping concepts: (1) learning disability; (2) learning difference; (3) learning difficulty; and (4) late development (also called "late bloomer"). In spite of the explosion of scientific discoveries about the physical causes for various types of LD, our culture will soon enter the 21st century without a commonly accepted definition of chronic learning difficulty that exists in 10% to 15% of the human population (Drake, 1989; Jordan, 1988, 1989, 1992; Rawson, 1988; Weisel, 1992).

Definitions of Learning Disability

The following definitions of LD illustrate the professional effort to define this phenomenon in our culture:

1962—Samuel Kirk

> A learning disability refers to a retardation, disorder, or delayed development in one or more of the processes of speech, language, reading, writing, arithmetic, or other school subjects resulting from a psychological handicap caused by a possible cerebral dysfunction and/or emotional or behavioral disturbances. It is not the result of mental retardation, sensory deprivation, or cultural and instructional factors (cited in Hammill, 1990).

1975—EDUCATION FOR ALL HANDICAPPED CHILDREN
(Public Law 94-142)

> Specific learning disability means a disorder in one or more of the basic pyschological processes involved in understanding or in using language spoken or written, which may manifest itself in an imperfect ability to listen, think, speak, read, write, spell, or to do mathematical calculations. The term includes such conditions as perceptual handicaps, brain injury, minimal brain dysfunction, dyslexia, and developmental aphasia. The term does not include children who have learning problems which are primarily the result of visual, hearing, or motor handicaps, of mental retardation, of emotional disturbance, or of environmental, cultural, or economic disadvantage (USOE, 1987, p. 65083)

1988—NATIONAL JOINT COMMITTEE ON LEARNING DISABILITIES

> Learning disabilities is a general term that refers to a heterogeneous group of disorders manifested by significant difficulties in acquisition and use of listening, speaking, reading, writing, reasoning or mathematical abilities. These disorders are intrinsic to the individual, pre-

sumed to be due to central nervous dysfunction, and may occur across the life span. . . . Although learning disabilities may occur concomitantly with other handicapping conditions (for example, sensory impairment, mental retardation, serious emotional disturbance) or with extrinsic influences (such as cultural differences, insufficient or inappropriate instruction), they are not the result of those conditions or influences (NJCLD, 1988, p.1).

WHAT CAUSES LEARNING DISABILITIES?

If there is no full agreement on the definition of LD, researchers are approaching agreement that learning disabilities are at least partly caused by physical differences in brain structure, genetic background, body chemistry, and right brain and midbrain structures. More than 100 years ago researchers learned that damage to certain regions of the left brain causes loss of language skills in speech, reading, and grammar. During the 1920s Orton's studies of brain-injured adults established the reality of trauma-induced LD. During the 1960s and 1970s, the extraordinary brain research at Harvard Medical School by Norman Geschwind, Walter Levitsky, and Albert Galaburda revealed that left brain pathways are different in dyslexic brains (Galaburda, 1983; Geschwind, 1984). By the mid-1980s it was clear that LD patterns originate in brain structure differences that are often passed down genetic lines in families (Jordan, 1989).

HOW THE BRAIN PROCESSES LANGUAGE INFORMATION

During the early 1980s the new science of brain imaging made it possible to watch the living brain at work in such tasks as reading, writing, listening to speech, doing arithmetic, analyzing words, and learning phonics. Through such brain imaging techniques as PET (positron emission tomography), MRI (magnetic resonance imaging), CT (computed tomography), and BEAM (brain electrical activity mapping), researchers discovered which regions of the left brain are primarily involved in

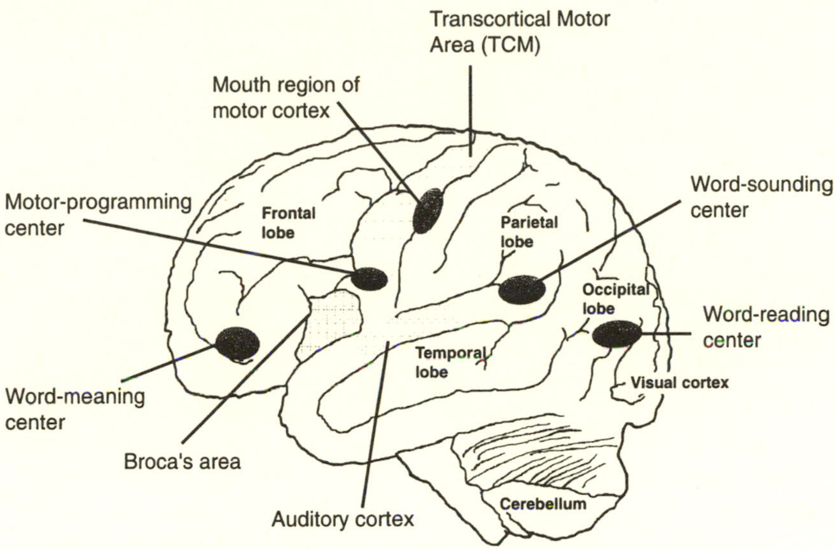

Figure 1.1 Regions of the left brain where language information is processed. Based upon brain imaging studies reported by Montgomery, 1989.

acquiring and practicing literacy skills (Montgomery, 1989). Figure 1.1 shows the regions of the left brain where most of the basic literacy skills develop. When these brain regions develop fully on schedule, the learner fluently absorbs and comprehends language skills as these left brain regions become interconnected and integrated. However, when nerve pathways within these brain regions develop differently or incompletely, a child, adolescent, or adult faces constant struggle in learning. LD is caused when specific neuronal pathways throughout the left cerebral cortex are too different or too incomplete to process language information fluently.

TYPES OF LD

Later chapters will show how certain kinds of differences in left brain pathways create patterns called dyslexia. Other kinds of neuronal pathway differences make it impossible for the person to master clear handwriting (*dysgraphia*). When still other regions of the left brain are formed differently, lifelong deficits in spelling and phonics (*dysorthographia*), as well as chronic struggle with arithmetic (*dyscalculia*) exist. When the cerebellum and certain regions of the left cerebral cortex are immature or incomplete, *attention deficit disorders* (ADHD and ADD) occur. When differences in midbrain and right brain structures are present, there are overlapping patterns of disruptive, oppositional, dyslogical, and immature behavior that complicate life for many persons who are LD.

The following chapters present simple ways to recognize specific types of LD in learners of all ages. Readers will learn to identify these forms of LD and will also study teaching and learning strategies that help learners with LD compensate effectively for learning differences. The first task for successful teaching of adults who are LD is to recognize the signs of learning disabilities. Then it is possible to match effective teaching and learning strategies to specific types of learning difficulties.

CHAPTER 2

Visual Perception Deficits

WORD BLINDNESS IN READING

In Chapter 1 I reviewed the discoveries by Berlin, Hinshelwood, and Orton of word blindness in bright students who had normal vision but who could not interpret symbols on the printed page. For more than 100 years professionals have continued to explore the mystery of why certain intelligent learners cannot decode what their eyes see on the printed page. Physicians who specialize in vision (ophthalmologists) have sought to separate diseases of the eye from this perplexing inability of healthy eyes to perceive printed symbols. The discipline of ophthalmology developed such strategies as patching (covering one eye) while using prism lenses and eye training exercises to decrease the word blind patterns described by Berlin, Hinshelwood, and Orton. Midway through this century a similar type of visual perception therapy emerged in the discipline of developmental optometry (Liesman, 1976). By combining a variety of corrective lenses with eye muscle training exercises, developmental optometry has sought to teach struggling readers how to overcome irregular eye teaming that is often found when learners cannot perceive printed symbols on the page. Both of these remedial approaches have helped struggling readers to overcome word blindness to some degree.

SACCADIC MOVEMENTS IN READING

During World War II Stanley Taylor pioneered a method of photographing eye movement patterns (*saccadic movements*) during the act of reading. Taylor's research documented the fact that persons who struggle to read usually have irregular, jerky eye muscle coordination (*poor saccads*). This irregular eye tracking keeps the eyes from aiming together as a team while the reader focuses and refocuses along lines of print (Taylor, 1960). However, these and many other efforts to improve reading ability through better vision did not answer the question: Why cannot intelligent learners with normal acuity see printed symbols on the page?

VISUAL PERCEPTION OVERLOAD

Irlen Procedure

The first step in answering this question emerged in 1976 when Helen Irlen discovered the role of color in treating reading disabilities in adults who were dyslexic. In working with several groups of struggling readers in California, Irlen noted that certain adults who had been diagnosed as dyslexic began to read more fluently when they covered book pages with transparent colored overlays. Some students immediately responded to yellow. Others responded to light green. Still others showed marked reading improvement with rose or peach or light blue. Over time Irlen developed the concept she first called *scotopic sensitivity syndrome*, now called *Irlen syndrome* (Irlen, 1991). This concept is concerned with the visual perception overload that occurs whenever the eyes concentrate upon black print on white paper under bright fluorescent light. Irlen's research identified several kinds of chronic visual perception patterns that occur when a struggling reader has scotopic sensitivity syndrome, or Irlen syndrome. Sometimes portions of the printed page pulse in and out of focus, as shown in Figure 2.1. Sometimes the outer edges of the page begin to swirl, as shown in Figure 2.2. Sometimes the interior regions of words fade away, as shown in Figure 2.3. Persons with severe Irlen syndrome have the visual perception impression that words stack on top of each other, then separate. The line below may suddenly move up to merge with the line being read, then move back down again. Sometimes words seem to slide or fall off the edges of the

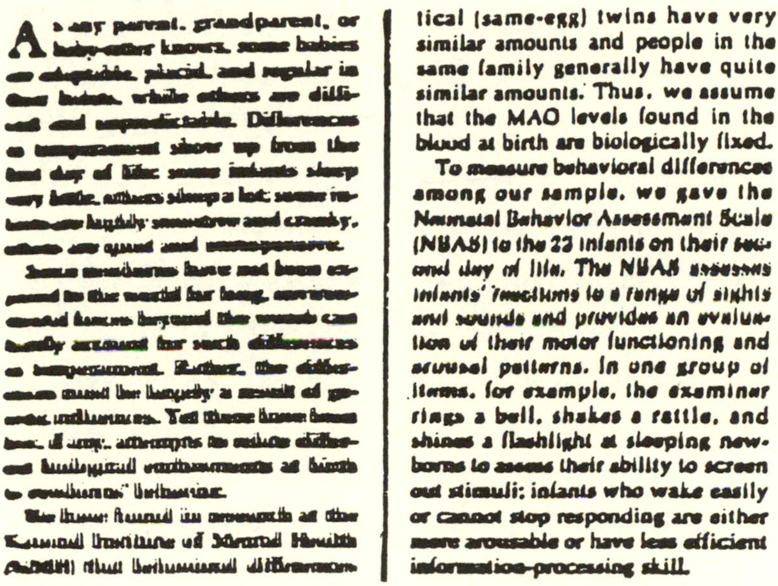
tical (same-egg) twins have very similar amounts and people in the same family generally have quite similar amounts. Thus, we assume that the MAO levels found in the blood at birth are biologically fixed.

To measure behavioral differences among our sample, we gave the Neonatal Behavior Assessment Scale (NBAS) to the 23 infants on their second day of life. The NBAS assesses infants' reactions to a range of sights and sounds and provides an evaluation of their motor functioning and arousal patterns. In one group of items, for example, the examiner rings a bell, shakes a rattle, and shines a flashlight at sleeping newborns to assess their ability to screen out stimuli; infants who wake easily or cannot stop responding are either more arousable or have less efficient information-processing skill.

Figure 2.1. Print pulses in and out of focus as persons with Irlen syndrome (scotopic sensitivity syndrome) look at black print on white paper.

page. Portions of the printed page may jiggle or rapidly blink on and off. Readers with these visual perception difficulties live with chronic headache across the forehead (frontal headache), across the temple regions (temporal headache), and down the back of the head (occipital headache). It is impossible for learners who have Irlen syndrome to continue to read longer than two or three minutes at one time. Eventually Irlen developed a process for coloring eye glasses, called Irlen filters, so that the struggling reader wears full-time color correction.

The Irlen procedure triggered a firestorm of controversy. In spite of criticism, this color correction strategy rapidly became a worldwide remedial practice with thousands of struggling readers showing significant improvement. The often dramatic reduction in word blindness when appropriate color is used made it increasingly clear that visual perception deficits in LD strugglers might indeed be related to some type of physical difference in how the brain processes visual information.

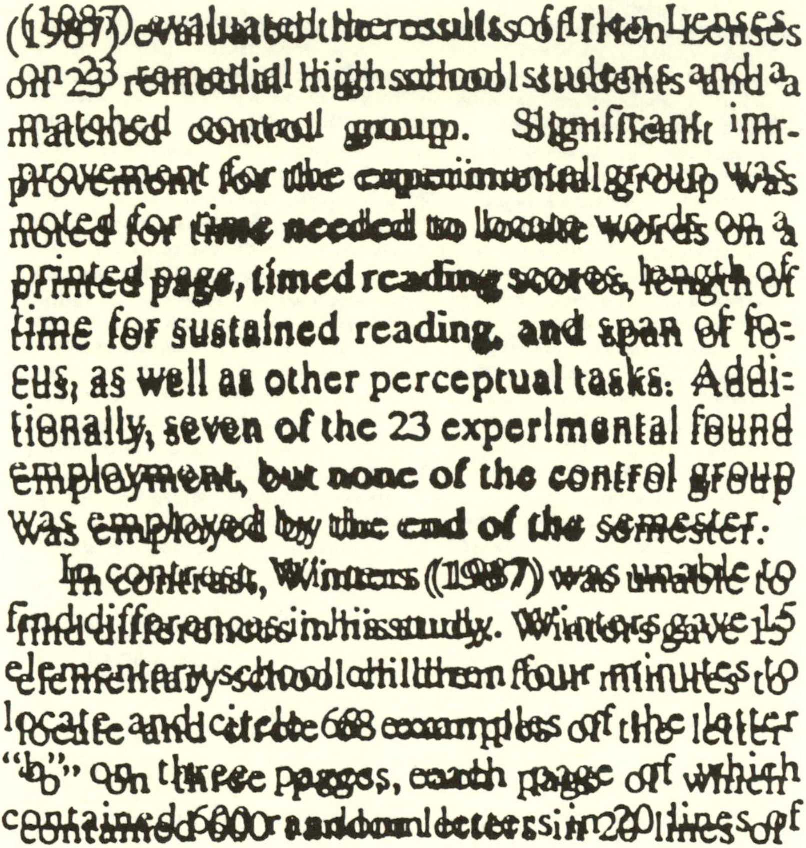

(1987) evaluated the results of Irlen Lenses
on 23 remedial high school students and a
matched control group. Significant improvement for the experimental group was
noted for time needed to locate words on a
printed page, timed reading scores, length of
time for sustained reading, and span of focus, as well as other perceptual tasks. Addi-
tionally, seven of the 23 experimental found
employment, but none of the control group
was employed by the end of the semester.
In contrast, Winters (1987) was unable to
find differences in his study. Winters gave 15
elementary school children four minutes to
locate and circle 68 examples of the letter
"b" on three pages, each page of which
contained 600 random letters in 20 lines of

Figure 2.2. Persons with Irlen syndrome often have the impression that the printed patterns around the edges of the central vision field are swirling.

Off-Center Central Vision

The second step in explaining word blindness appeared in 1987 when Geiger and Lettvin published their research of off-center foveal structures in the retina of adults who are severely dyslexic (Geiger & Lettvin, 1987). This off-center foveal condition produces irregular central vision patterns. Geiger and Lettvin demonstrated why many poor readers cannot read by looking

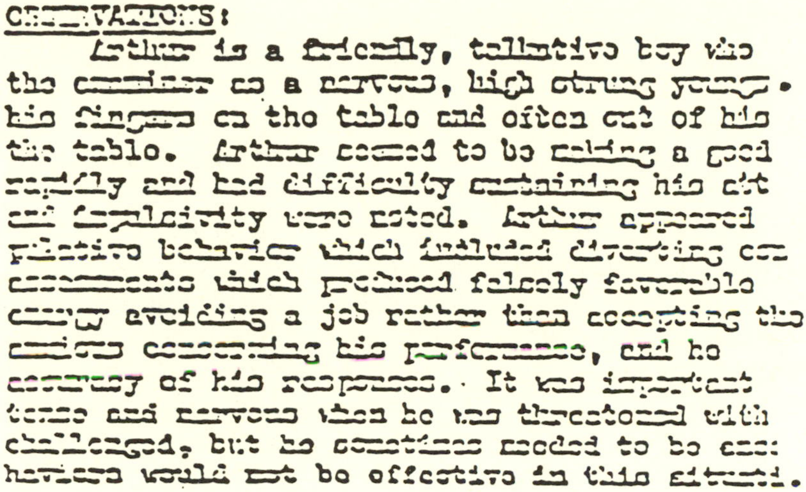

Figure 2.3. Persons with Irlen syndrome often see the inside details of printed words fade away, then return off and on in cycles. Irlen calls this the "washout effect."

straight at the printed page. Within seconds after they concentrate central vision upon black print on white paper, these readers become word blind and must glance away. From that point of visual perception burnout, they are forced to use the edges of their vision (*peripheral vision*) if they are to keep on reading. These strugglers must rapidly glance at constantly changing angles to see clearly. If they keep looking straight ahead, their central vision suddenly becomes blurred. Geiger and Lettvin demonstrated that using large card markers with slots cut out reduced deterioration of visual perception and permitted these readers to stay longer with the printed page. This research added a second piece to the puzzle of why certain intelligent persons cannot read if they look straight at the printed page.

Incomplete Cell Development

A third step in solving the puzzle of word blindness appeared in 1991 when Livingstone, Rosen, Drislane and Galaburda announced their discoveries of abnormal cell development along the neuronal pathways that link the retina and the visual cortex (Livingstone et al., 1991). In 1993 this discovery was corroborated by Lehmkuhle, Garzia, Turner, Hash, and Baro (1993) at the University of Missouri School of Optometry. Specialists in brain research have discovered several "information highways" throughout both brain hemispheres that transfer data from where it is received to where that information is processed. Livingstone, Lehmkuhle, and their colleagues have documented a specific type of incomplete cell formation within the optic pathway that links the retina to the visual cortex. Figure 2.4 shows a diagram of the two kinds of visual perception cells that work as a team. The large cells, called magno cells, rapidly transfer portions of eyesight information to the visual cortex where visual perception occurs. At the same time, strings of small cells, called parvo cells, more slowly transfer the rest of the eyesight information to the visual cortex. When all of these cells are fully developed, visual perception data passes smoothly from the eyes to the visual cortex. The brain instantly perceives what the eyes just saw. The studies by Livingstone et al. and Lehmkuhle et al. revealed that many struggling readers cannot recognize printed symbols because the large (magno) cells are incompletely developed. This deficit in cell formation prevents the faster information bits from reaching the visual cortex at the right time. Instead of seeing a clear, complete image, the brain perceives blurred, incomplete images that behave the way Irlen's research described.

HOW MANY WORD BLIND LEARNERS ARE THERE?

Numerous studies have attempted to find out how many LD learners struggle with these kinds of visual perception deficits. Jordan has estimated that 65% of all dyslexic strugglers are handicapped by forms of word blindness (Jordan, 1988, 1989). Nancie Payne and associates have found that 3 out of 5

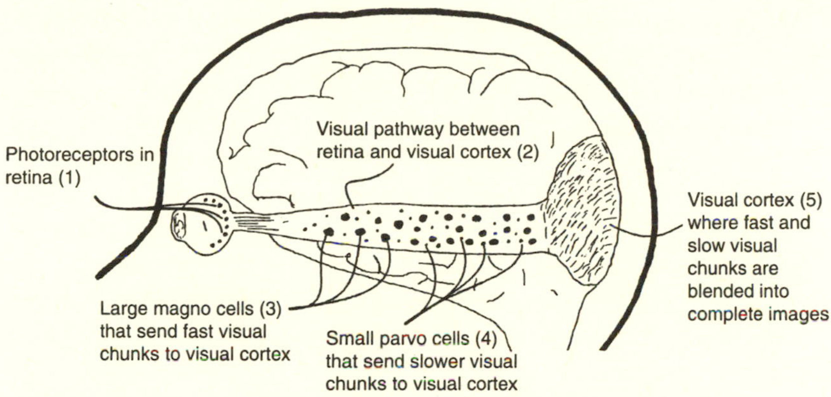

Figure 2.4. In reading and general seeing, light is absorbed by the photoreceptors in the retina (1). That visual information then passes along the visual pathway (2) to the visual cortex (5) where the brain interprets what is seen. Two types of cells carry visual information from the retina to the visual cortex. Large magno cells (3) process part of the visual information rapidly. Small parvo cells (4) process the rest of the visual information more slowly. These bundles of fast and slow visual information are blended by the visual cortex to create meaningful images. Livingstone et al. (1991) discovered that the magno cells in many poor readers are underdeveloped.

dyslexic adults in the workplace display significant problems with visual perception (Payne, 1993). Weisel has found more than half of adult dyslexics manifesting problems with visual perception in reading (Weisel, 1992). Pollan and Williams have reported that 45% of dyslexic students in the high school drop-out population display word blind characteristics (Pollan & Williams, 1992). Irlen reports a worldwide ratio of 3 out of 5 struggling readers who cannot cope with black print on white paper under fluorescent light (personal communication, September 12, 1993). It is clear that the issue of LD by whatever name includes chronic struggle with visual perception. This factor must be addressed before those with learning disabilities can benefit from typical remedial procedures.

CHAPTER 3

How to Compensate for Visual Perception Deficits

THE IMPACT OF VISUAL PERCEPTION DEFICITS

In Chapter 2 I presented examples of what the brain perceives when students with deficits in visual perception try to read black print on white paper. Within a very brief time the reader is overwhelmed by blurring of the print, movement of letters or words on the page, the impression that details are pulsing in and out of focus, or the sensation that words are falling off the page. Once this breakdown in visual perception begins, the reader has no choice but to look away from the page and stop trying to read. It is not always possible for instructors or tutors to send such struggling readers to a vision specialist who can correct these patterns. Going through a full diagnostic procedure that ends with prism lenses or colored Irlen filters costs several hundred dollars. Struggling adults who need this correction cannot always afford such treatment. Nevertheless, by doing certain things with struggling readers, it is usually possible to double or triple the time these learners can work with black print on white pages at little expense. Reducing the impact of poor visual perception begins by breaking reading tasks into small segments. It is impossible for word blind learners to keep on using their vision without taking many brief vacations from reading, copying, looking at a computer screen, or marking bubbles on seperate answer sheets.

LEVEL OF LIGHT

One of the most critical factors in compensating for poor visual perception is the light in the work space. Overhead fluorescent lights are the most significant culprit for word blind persons (Irlen 1991; Jordan, 1988, 1989). The first step in compensating for deficits in visual perception is to adjust the light by which students read, copy, and do written work. Instructors must watch closely for the degree of stress that is triggered by light in the learning situation. Not all students who have trouble reading are equally sensitive to light. The following severity scale shows the range of light sensitivity found among the 90 million adults in our workforce who have low literacy skills:

0	1 2 3	4 5 6 7	8 9 10
no problem with light	some problems with overhead light	constant problems with overhead light	severe problems with overhead light

Level 0: No Problem with Light

Some adults who struggle to read, copy, and write show no signs of being sensitive to overhead fluorescent light. Nor do they experience the visual perceptual distortions of black print on white paper as shown in Figures 2.1, 2.2, and 2.3. Chapter 4 will present other LD patterns that may be the reason for poor reading ability. Instructors and tutors can determine this difference by asking struggling learners whether bright light bothers their eyes while reading, copying, writing, or working at a computer screen. The instructor also asks students to describe how print appears on the page to determine if they see the patterns shown in Figures 2.1, 2.2, and 2.3. Level 0 means no consistent problems with the level of light or with distortions of print on the page.

Level 1, 2, 3: Some Problems with Overhead Light

A student who has only some problems with overhead light will display certain behaviors while reading, copying, writing, or looking at a computer screen:

- Frequently glances away, then looks back at printed or written work.
- Often brushes at eyes or rubs eyes lightly.
- Frequently glances at the light source with a small frown.
- Often squirms as if trying to become more comfortable.
- Continually changes body posture by leaning closer, leaning back, turning sideways, turning the book or work page to different angles.
- Shows concern with time. Wonders how much more work is yet to be done.
- Does not keep on doing visual work. Often stops to rest eyes.
- After prolonged visual work, comments about eyes being tired or headache developing.
- Attempts to shade book or work pages from overhead light.
- Frequently loses the place, then touches the page or computer screen to find the place again.
- Occasionally comments that print is getting blurry.

Students at Level 1, 2, or 3 have compensated all their lives for these mild visual perception deficits. They are seldom aware that they are overly sensitive to bright light or that they must work around visual distortions as they read, copy, write, or sit at a computer. These persons assume that everyone sees the way they do.

Level 4, 5, 6, 7: Constant Problems with Overhead Light

A student who has constant problems with overhead light will display the following behavior patterns:

- Wants to wear a bill cap indoors with bill turned forward to shade the eyes.

- Habitually shades book or work pages by leaning forward over the work space.
- Often cups a hand against the forehead to shade face and eyes.
- Whispers or mumbles to self while doing visual work.
- Guides eyes by touching the work page.
- Yawns frequently while reading to relieve tension.
- Continually changes body posture by turning sideways, leaning forward, leaning back.
- Continually moves book or work pages to a new angle.
- Raises book or work page up close to eyes, then moves it back to desk top.
- Continually glances away from work to let eyes rest.
- Frequently rubs at eyes or wipes away tears.
- Shows continual concern for time. Wants vision work to be finished.
- Welcomes interruptions that let eyes leave the work page.
- Eyes stay on printed material for only brief periods of time.

Level 8, 9, 10:
Severe Problems with Overhead Light

A student who has severe problems with overhead light will display the following behavior patterns:

- Squints painfully with immediate watering of the eyes.
- Refuses to keep on looking at black print on white paper.
- Feels immediate headache around the eyes and across the forehead.
- Rapidly develops headache across the temples and down the back of head and neck.
- Sees massive distortion of printed pages: details pulsing; print appearing smudged; words moving; lines moving; words sliding off the page; edges swirling; details flickering or disappearing; details fading, then coming back; words stacking on top of each other.
- Has very brief span of seeing print clearly.

- Immediately, constantly loses the place on the page or computer screen.
- Wants low, indirect light in work space.
- Switches back and forth from looking straight ahead to looking sideways in rapid glances.

INDIRECT LIGHT

Students who display these patterns above Level 5 must have modified light in order to cope with the visual demands of reading, copying, writing, and computer processing. Instructors and tutors must experiment with indirect light to find what is best for each student. Sometimes a small table lamp with a 60 or 75 watt frosted bulb is best. Occasionally a student who is light sensitive prefers a small halogen lamp that shines a spotlight onto the work page with no other light coming from the periphery. In a classroom with overhead fluorescent lights, these sensitive students often can cope if half of the overhead lights are turned off, leaving part of the room in soft shadows. If the study area has outside windows, it is usually best to turn off all indoor lights and let students work by indirect light from outdoors. Students who are sensitive to light must be allowed to make their own decisions about how the study space is to be lighted.

SIZE OF PRINT

Most students who rank above Level 5 on the severity scale prefer large print with extra space between the lines; however, it is not always possible for instructors to find textbooks and other prepared materials that offer large print with separated lines. Most learning centers have word processors that allow instructors to develop individualized work pages with larger print and extra spacing. Tutors and instructors should experiment with a variety of print sizes, letting students choose the most comfortable format for reading. Figure 3.1 shows examples of print sizes and spacing formats that usually reduce visual perception stress.

COLORED OVERLAYS

In Chapter 2 I reviewed Irlen's research that led to the use of colored page overlays for struggling readers. The Irlen procedure of diagnosing which color or combination of colors, as described in Irlen's book *Reading by the Colors*, is not always available or affordable for struggling readers. When this level of expert remediation is not available, instructors must do the next best thing. It is not difficult to find transparent colored materials that can be used as page overlays. Nevertheless, it is critical that shiny, brightly colored plastic not be used. The colored gel filters used in theater lighting are often good for page overlays. Soft pastel colors of light blue, pale yellow, rose, or light green that do not cast a shiny reflection should be used to cover reading pages and computer screens. No two light-sensitive students have the same response to colored overlays. Occasionally a light-sensitive struggling reader does not respond to any color that is applied to the page. Some persons need to make a "sandwich" with two or more colors stacked together. Sometimes an individual needs 2, 3, or 4 layers of the same color to achieve full benefit. For those who respond well to colored overlay application, dramatic improvement in reading is often seen.

COLORED PAPER

Those who struggle with faulty visual perception usually respond well when reading materials are printed on colored paper. Even when colored overlays have no benefit in reading, writing on colored paper or reading from colored pages reduces vision stress for light-sensitive students. Every learning center should have a variety of softly colored paper for copying, doing math, and writing essays. Work pages should be printed on a

10-point type in newspaper

Thunderstorms and flooding swept across Dallas on Saturday, causing extensive street flooding and evacuations.

12-point type double spaced

Thunderstorms and flooding

swept across Dallas on Satur-

day, causing extensive street

14-point type 1 1/2 space

Thunderstorms and

flooding swept across

Dallas on Saturday

18-point type 1 1/2

Thunderstorms and

swept across Dallas

20-point type 1 1/2 spaced

Thunderstorms and flooding

swept across Dallas on Satur-

Figure 3.1. Most persons who struggle with reading need larger type size and wider spacing between lines to maintain clear visual perception and to keep the place.

variety of softly colored paper. Bright, glaring paper should be avoided. The instructor's goal should be to avoid black print on white paper as much as possible for learners whose literacy skills are behind schedule. Students who are sensitive to light should choose which color they prefer in work paper. Sometimes pink or yellow overloads the eyes for certain students. Instructors should provide a variety of tinted paper to let readers choose the most comfortable color.

USING MARKERS

A major problem for students who have visual perception deficits is seeing too much at one time. These students are immediately overwhelmed when the edges of their vision are too crowded while they concentrate on central vision images. These learners can reduce visual frustration and increase central vision skills by masking the edges of their vision. Many struggling readers automatically try to mask by placing one hand above or below the line they are reading. They often run a finger below or a thumb above the line as they read. Some readers use two fingers to frame words and syllables. Others lay a pencil below the line to guide the eyes along the line. Some persons fold a piece of paper and cover the lower part of the page with the marker lying just below the line being read. A more efficient marking strategy is to make page markers that cover as much of the page as the student needs to mask. These markers should be made from softly colored material that is comfortable for the student's vision. In Chapter 2 I presented Geiger and Lettvin's research that described the value of using markers with slots cut out. These researchers discovered that reading can be enhanced for many struggling readers if only part of a line is seen while the rest of the print is hidden by the marker (Figure 3.2 and Figure 3.3). Research has shown that using markers often doubles or triples the reading stamina for students who have fragile visual perception patterns (Geiger & Lettvin, 1987; Jordan, 1988, 1898; Weisel, 1992).

OPEN SPACING

Open spacing is critical for students who struggle with poor visual perception. Figure 3.4 shows examples of open

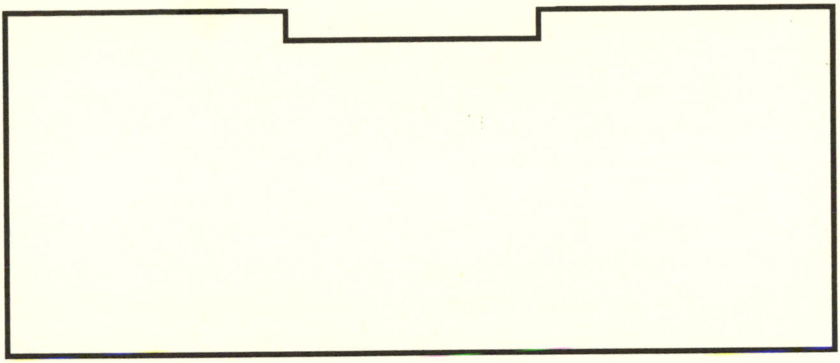

Figure 3.2. Struggle to keep the eyes focused on the right place in reading can be reduced by using a card marker with a slot cut out on the top edge. The reader sees only the print in the center of the visual field. The reader's eyes are not overwhelmed by too much detail on the edges.

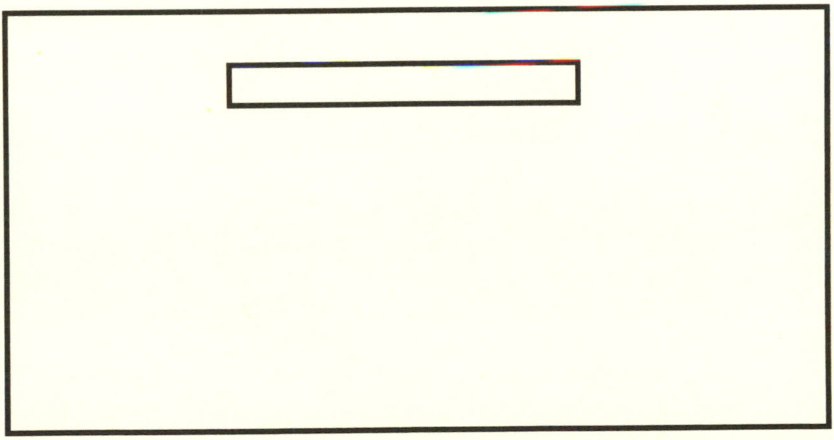

Figure 3.3. Some readers have better visual perception control if they use a card with a slot cut out inside.

spacing that greatly enhances reading for most adults who have limited literacy skills. Open spacing is equally important for writing. Persons who rank above Level 5 on the light sensitivity severity scale should skip lines as they write and copy. Instructors should require that all written work, including math and

10-point type with no extra space between words and lines

The world has always been in a state of change. Some changes have been good for the society, but many changes have harmed the environment and many species of wildlife.

12-point type with extra space between words and lines

The world has always been in a state of change. Some changes have been good for the society, but many changes have harmed the environment and many species of wildlife.

14-point with double space between words and lines

The world has always been in a state of change. Some changes have been good for the society, but many changes have harmed the environment and many species of wildlife.

Figure 3.4. Providing double space between words and lines allows many struggling readers to stay much longer with reading. Word recognition is better, and comprehension improves.

arithmetic, be double or triple spaced. As the work page becomes filled with writing, open spacing allows the student more easily to review what he or she has just encoded. When printed book pages or handwritten work pages are overcrowded, the student encounters the same kind of visual perception burnout we have seen with black print on white paper under bright light.

PLENTY OF TIME

Students who display light sensitivity or who struggle with visual perception above Level 4 on the severity scale cannot read or write in a hurry. It is physically impossible for them to stay in control of the factors discussed in this chapter. Without warning every few seconds, what they see is momentarily out of focus or appears distorted. These struggling learners have no choice but to pause, glance away, and let their visual processing return to normal. If other types of LD are also present, having to hurry through reading, copying, or writing activities overwhelms the students' skills and knowledge. Pressing these strugglers to hurry triggers anxiety that often escalates into intense phobia. At that point the individual quits trying and may not return to the learning situation.

CHAPTER 4

Visual Dyslexia

DOES DYSLEXIA EXIST?

Historians of the next century will note with some surprise that one of the great educational controversies of the 20th century was whether dyslexia is myth or reality. From 1884 when Berlin first described dyslexia, professionals from many disciplines have disagreed. In 1982 Martha Evans published an exhaustive review of the literature related to this issue. Evans found more than 2,200 reputable works devoted to describing dyslexia (Evans, 1982). By 1994 the number of published works about dyslexia had more than doubled. In 1985 Drake Duane, then a neurologist with the Mayo Clinic, stated: "Dyslexia is the most thoroughly researched of all forms of learning disability" (Duane, 1985). In the two decades from 1965–1985 such notable scientists as Geschwind, Levitsky, and Galaburda reported their anatomical studies of dyslexic brains. They had found specific neuronal differences in adult males who had been poor readers (Geschwind & Levitsky, 1968; Galaburda, 1985). In 1985 it was discovered that some forms of dyslexia are linked to Chromosome 15 in the DNA chain within certain families (Jordan, 1989). In 1994, the Institute for Behavioral Genetics in Colorado reported that some forms of dyslexia appear to be linked to Chromosome 6 (personal communication, October 4, 1994). Scores of prominent persons have told their stories of lifelong struggle with dyslexia (Jordan, 1989). Yet as we approach the 21st century, many educators insist that dyslexia is a separate issue not worth considering in adult education. As Carolyn Buell Kidder reported in 1991, it is not uncommon to hear reading specialists declare that dyslexia rarely exists, if at all, among low-literacy adults (Kidder, 1991). With the enormous volume of research and explanatory writing about dyslexia available today, it is difficult to understand why the existance of dyslexia remains a controversial issue.

WHAT IS DYSLEXIA?

The first research of dyslexia focused upon struggle to read or to interpret printed symbols. It was first believed that dyslexia only involved turning letters backward or upside down, or scrambling the sequence of printed letters while reading from a page. This simplistic point of view guided Berlin and Hinshelwood in their 19th-century work with word blindness. This limited point of view also guided Orton in his 1920s research of strephosymbolia (twisted symbols). The landmark anatomical studies of Geschwind, Levitsky, and Galaburda broadened the recognition that dyslexia involves much more than just perceiving letters backward or upside down. In 1987 the Texas State Legislature mandated that every child in the Texas public schools should be evaluated for dyslexia. The following simple definition guided this legislation:

> Dyslexia is a disorder of constitutional origin manifested by difficulty in learning to read, write or spell, despite conventional instruction, adequate intelligence, and sociocultural opportunity (HB 157, 1985, p. 2).

In 1988 Margaret Rawson published her intriguing collection of essays titled *The Many Faces of Dyslexia* in which she explored the myriad ways dyslexia is manifested in struggling learners. Rawson described the impact of dyslexia in every area of academic learning and social development (Rawson, 1988).

Carl Drake (1989) presented a simple description of dyslexia:

> Dyslexia has been defined in many ways. Dyslexia is an invisible handicap that prevents people from learning language skills through traditional methods. It is not related to intellectual ability. An estimated ten

> percent of the population is affected to some degree by dyslexia. For each female with dyslexia approximately five males are affected. Sometimes thought to be simply a "reading problem," dyslexia may affect a range of language and information processing skills, including spelling, handwriting, composition, study skills, mathematics, and foreign languages. (p. 6)

In 1989 Jordan summarized the global problems of dyslexia:

> Dyslexia is a cluster of factors that keeps an intelligent person from learning how to do school work successfully. As dyslexic students move upward through the grades, they do not develop fluent skills in reading from printed materials. They cannot write effectively. Penmanship is poor. Sentence structure is ragged and incomplete. These students usually have trouble copying accurately from the chalkboard or from a book. They seldom do well with basic arithmetic. They must count fingers to add, subtract, multiply, or divide. They usually need to whisper over and over while their fingers touch or handle the work page. Rate of work is usually very slow. These students become intensely frustrated if teachers try to make them work faster. Their eyes become overly tired after a few minutes of close work. Their ability to see details clearly at desk-top level deteriorates. Attention span is often very short, causing them to dart off on rabbit trails instead of keeping the attention focused fully on the task. These students listen poorly. They cannot keep up with a flow of oral information. They often cannot follow directions that involve memory for left and right, or north, east, south, west. They are often much less mature than their age-mates, which creates continual conflict with peers and leaders. These struggling learners do very poorly on tests, especially when time is limited. They are frequently misdiagnosed as being mentally retarded or emotionally disturbed because they cannot always give coherent standard responses on diagnostic tests. (p. 8)

TYPES OF DYSLEXIA

Jordan (1972, 1988, 1989) has defined three types of dyslexia that are commonly found in health therapy and educational programs. Much of the controversy surrounding the issue of dyslexia stems from the fact that early research of this problem was associated with persons who had suffered some form of brain injury. Educators who reject the concept of dyslexia often view the issue through the perspective of damage to the brain. As previously mentioned, such a point of view is outdated.

TRAUMA-INDUCED DYSLEXIA

A relatively rare form of dyslexia is called *trauma induced dyslexia.* This type of dyslexia is caused by injury or damage to regions of the brain where literacy skills develop. Sometimes such injury occurs before birth through nutritional deficiencies during pregnancy or exposing the fetus to harmful substances during the early stages of nerve development. Head injuries on the job or sports accidents sometimes damage portions of the left brain where language processing occurs. Drug overdose or poisoning can destroy the myelin sheath surrounding nerve pathways in the language regions of the brain. Stroke, aneurism, or cerebral hemorrhage may destroy vital nerve pathways involved with reading, spelling, speaking, or writing. In older persons, degenerative brain syndromes such as Alzheimer's disease gradually destroy language processing centers. These kinds of trauma to brain structures produce dyslexic patterns that did not exist before the accident or illness. It is estimated that 3 out of 1,000 persons are afflicted by trauma-induced dyslexia (Jordan, 1988, 1989). Health professionals in occupational therapy or physical therapy are more likely to see this type of dyslexia than are classroom teachers.

PRIMARY DYSLEXIA

As Berlin (1884), Hinshelwood (1900), Orton (1925), Jordan (1972, 1988, 1989), Duane (1983), Rawson (1988), Weisel (1992), Payne (1993), Pollan and Williams (1992), and others have described, approximately 5 out of 100 persons of all ages have chronic, lifelong struggle at a deep level with literacy skills. In spite of being intelligent, these individuals cannot master basic skills of reading, spelling, writing, and arithmetic. This chronic struggle with literacy learning is called *primary dyslexia.* This LD pattern is also called *deep dyslexia.* No matter how hard they try or what teaching methods are used, these individuals do not master basic literacy skills above upper 3rd-grade to middle 4th-grade levels. Yet they are often well above average in intelligence. This form of dyslexia is linked to differences in genetic structure (chromosomes 6 and 15). This LD syndrome runs down the family line from one generation to the next. Primary dyslexia is found nine times more often in males than in females (Jordan, 1988, 1989). It sometimes skips generations with the mother not being dyslexic but with older male relatives and a son or daughter being dyslexic. Primary dyslexia does not diminish or disappear with age. As the child with deep dyslexia passes through adolescence into adulthood, dyslexic patterns do not go away. In studying families of primary dyslexics, Geschwind (1984) found that relatives are four times more likely to be left handed (13%) than the general population (3%). Relatives of primary dyslexics tend to become white haired or gray haired very early, starting in late teens or early twenties. These relatives also have many more allergies than most families. They suffer from chronic digestive problems, including gastritis, irritable bowel syndrome, Chron's disease, excessive flatulance, and trouble digesting milk products. Relatives of primary dyslexics frequently suffer from autoimmune disorders such as lupus, fibromyalgia, and arthritis (Geschwind, 1984; Galaburda, 1983).

DEVELOPMENTAL DYSLEXIA

The most commonly seen type of dyslexia is called by two names: *developmental dyslexia* or *secondary dyslexia.* Approximately 10 out of 100 persons manifest this LD syndrome (Drake, 1989; Jordan, 1989, 1989; Weisel, 1992). At early school ages, it may not be possible to tell whether a child will be primary dyslexic or secondary dyslexic later on. As the child reaches certain developmental milestones, the severity of this type of dyslexia begins to diminish. There is noticeable improvement in literacy skills during early adolescence, midway through puberty, during late adolescence, and in early years of adulthood. The individual never fully outgrows all of the dyslexic patterns, but the level of severity gradually declines as body changes occur during adolescence and early adulthood.

LEVEL OF SEVERITY

The following severity scale shows the range of struggle that dyslexic learners face:

1	2	3	4	5	6	7	8	9	10
	mild			moderate				severe	

Primary dyslexia (deep dyslexia) is always at the severe range of struggle, regardless of the age of the learner. However, secondary dyslexia (developmental dyslexia) diminishes steadily as physical maturation occurs. At age 7 the dyslexic child may be at level 8 in his or her struggle with academic learning. By age 11 when the first hormone production triggers the onset of puberty, the child may be down to level 7 in learning difficulty. By age 15, after three years or so of adolescent development, dyslexic patterns may have diminished to level 6. This gradual decline in dyslexic struggle continues through late adolescence and into early adulthood. By age 22 this dyslexic learner may be down to level 4 or level 3 in LD patterns.

VISUAL DYSLEXIA

Within the overall LD condition called dyslexia are several subtypes of learning difficulty. One of the prominent forms of this learning disability is *visual dyslexia.* This does not refer to problems in seeing. It is true that many LD learners have the visual perceptual patterns described in Chapter 2. As many as 65% of primary dyslexic learners suffer from Irlen syndrome or

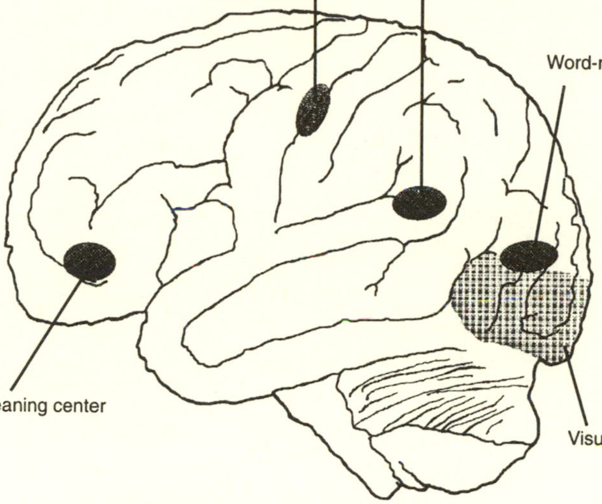

Figure 4.1. Regions of the left brain where visual dyslexia occurs. Bridges are out between the language-processing centers where sounds are connected to letters and speech patterns are produced.

other types of visual perception deficits (Jordan, 1988, 1989). However, visual dyslexia has nothing to do with the eyes. Visual dyslexia occurs in the visual cortex where the brain interprets and processes what the eyes see. Figure 4.1 shows the regions of the left brain where visual dyslexia occurs. Numerous nerve pathways inside and between the visual cortex, auditory cortex, word analysis center, word-speaking center, handwriting-control center, and word-meaning center are incompletely developed. Many of these nerve pathways have overly wide gaps between synapse junctions that prevent transmission of thought patterns. Dendrite pruning is erratic and often leaves too many dendrites in the wrong places within the synapse pathways. It is like having too many bridges out as well as too many overlapping pathways along the "information highways" of the brain. Visual dyslexia is caused by nerve pathway deficits within and adjacent to the visual cortex of the left brain.

Word seen on card	Student's Matching Choice from Memory					
	saw two alike					
barn	bran	pran	puar	bnar	narb	uarp	barn
spot	spot	tobs	tops	stop	stob	sbot	tods
silver	sliver	silver	vilser	revils	revlis	selvir	verlis
				saw two alike			
trap	trad	brat	rapt	part	prat	bart	trap
must	tums	tsum	smut	swnt	tsuw	must	wnst
severe	severe	reverse	esrever	eversen	severe	neverse	nervese
	saw two alike						
sheep	sheeb	speeh	sheed	sdeey	sheep	speey	peehs
trash	tarsh	shraf	farsh	shart	trash	frash	sharf
wash	mash	sham	wash	shaw	whas	hsaw	sahw

Figure 4.2. Visual dyslexia is seen in scrambled sequence of letters, reading words backwards, seeing different patterns but thinking they are the same, and so forth. This test comes from the *Jordan Prescriptive Tutorial Reading Program* (1988).

CONFUSION OF SYMBOLS

A major characteristic of visual dyslexia is the habit of turning printed symbols backward or upside down, as well as scrambling details out of correct sequence. Figure 4.2 shows examples of how visual dyslexia interferes when the student tries to match words and numbers. Symbol confusion is also seen when dyslexic learners write from memory. Figure 4.3 shows the struggle of visual dyslexia as the person tries to write the alphabet from memory. Figure 4.4 shows visual dyslexic strug-

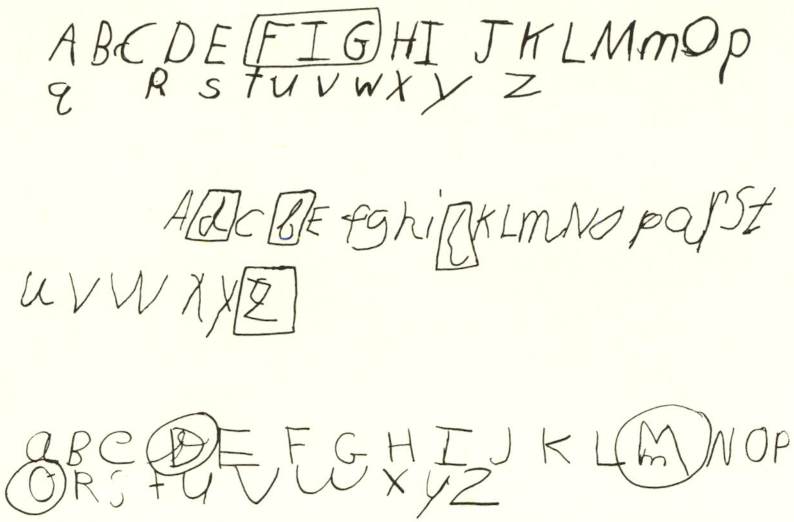

Figure 4.3. Writing the alphabet from memory brings underlying dyslexia to the surface. The alphabet sequence is often scrambled or incomplete. Letters are often turned backward. The person shows confusion between capital and lower case letters. Uneven spacing between letters indicates poor visual perception in controlling pencil movement. Letter size fluctuates. However, these three adults are above average in intelligence.

gle in such sequential memory activities as writing the days of the week and months of the year from memory.

The simplest, most direct way to find visual dyslexia is to have the student write the alphabet, days of the week, and months of the year from memory (Jordan, 1988, 1989; Pollan & Williams, 1992; Weisel, 1992). The student should write on lined paper with no printed material on the walls of the room to give clues. If an intelligent person who has attended school for several years produces work like Figure 4.3 and Figure 4.4, it is safe to conclude that the individual is dyslexic.

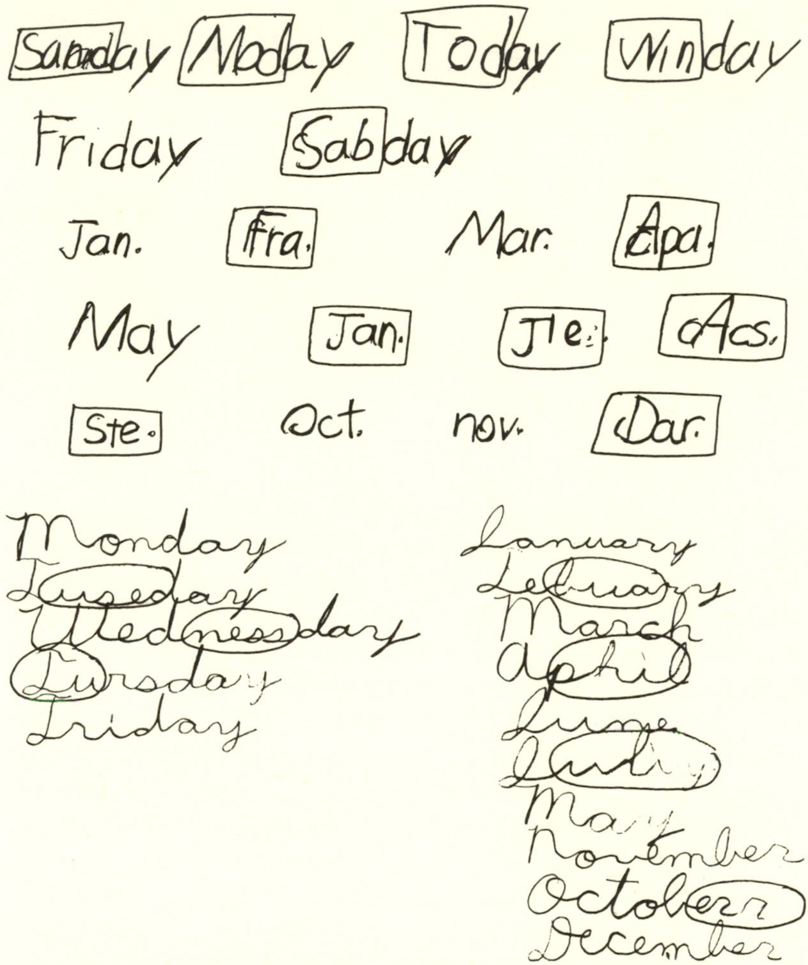

Figure 4.4. Writing the days of the week and months of the year brings underlying dyslexia to the surface. Persons who are dyslexic struggle with this task as these examples illustrate.

CHAPTER 5

How to Compensate for Visual Dyslexia

LEFT-TO-RIGHT, TOP-TO-BOTTOM ORIENTATION

The written language of every culture is built upon a specific perceptual orientation. All languages of European origin that use variations of the Roman alphabet (English, Spanish, French, Italian, German, and so forth) assume that reading and writing will follow a basic directional orientation: left to right, top to bottom. Within these language cultures, academic programs assume that students will automatically follow this perceptual orientation in decoding and encoding language symbols. If reading, writing, and spelling do not follow this left-to-right, top-to-bottom orientation, constant mistakes are made in word analysis, spelling, word recognition, and communication. Other language cultures often have an opposite perceptual orientation with written language interpreted right to left, top to bottom. Or language symbols may flow bottom to top, right to left. Within the culture of standard English literacy, all persons must automatically process left to right, top to bottom, or else they are regarded as being literacy failures.

SCRAMBLED PERCEPTUAL ORIENTATION

The essential difference in dyslexia is that left brain language centers do not learn automatic directional orientation, whatever the language culture may be. Regardless of cultural origin, certain individuals do not develop automatic language symbol processing. To be dyslexic is to go through frequent cycles of scrambling the sequence, reversing details, turning things upside down, and starting at the wrong end of words and working backward the opposite way. Unfortunately, persons with dyslexia cannot predict when these differences will occur.

BACKWARD LETTERS AND NUMBERS

For example in the English language, on one line of print the reader who is dyslexic may see *baby*. On the next line the same word may look like dady or paby or papy. In handling numbers, the person with dyslexia never knows when 37 may flip to 73 or a phone number may be transposed from 654-3827 to 456-3728. In traveling Interstate Highway 40 from Little Rock, Arkansas, to Amarillo, Texas, drivers encounter three exit signs: Altus Tulsa Altus. How can the bewildered driver who is dyslexic ever be sure which city he or she has reached?

LIFELONG COMPENSATION

Living with visual dyslexia requires lifelong compensation. Every successful person who is dyslexic develops a repertoire of compensation clues that work most of the time. The most critical compensation strategy is to remember where to start. To be successful in this left-to-right, bottom-to-top culture, persons with dyslexia must develop rapid rehearsal techniques that place them quickly at the correct starting place. Those who live with the scrambling/reversing/rotating perceptions of visual dyslexia must learn how to run through a short list of orientation clues: "OK, where do I start? Let's see, where is left? Ok, now where is top? Which way do I go next? Oh, there it is. Ok, now let's see. Ooops! Start over. Now I've got it. OK, now try again." This quick litany is repeated over and over in every situation that threatens to swamp the dyslexic person in another episode of losing one's way in language processing. Individuals who are dyslexic often describe this perceptual challenge as like standing in a boat that is about to tip over and dump them into the water.

DIRECTIONAL MARKERS

The challenge for instructors and learners who are dyslexic is to develop a simple system of directional markers that guide scrambled or reversed perceptions to the correct starting point. Sometimes these markers can be visible. Often these markers must be invisible. Always these markers involve some degree of touching or pointing to guide the person's attention to the correct location.

Where Is Left?

Beginning in childhood, learners with dyslexia wrestle with the challenge of remembering left and right. Adults who have not yet mastered this orientation must practice finding left. In all reading and writing tasks, left can be marked on the page so that the eyes immediately locate the marker. A dot, a star, a spot of color, or any type of visible marker will do. The person learns to find that left marker before starting to do the paper task. In numbered tasks, such as arithmetic, the learner who is dyslexic must also pay attention to numerical order. The hazard in following number sequence is the tendency to read 9 for 6, 3 for E, 5 for 2, 7 for L, 21 for 12, 31 for 13, and so forth. Visual dyslexia involves chronic, unpredictable cycles of losing left-to-right, top-to-bottom orientation. The most dependable visible cue for locating left is a mark, a dot, or a spot of color that is distinctly different from the rest of the work page. The eyes quickly locate this marker to prevent lost time and buildup of frustration.

Where Is Top?

After locating left, the learner with dyslexia must also locate top. As simple as this procedure seems to be, most persons who are dyslexic must go through a two-step process of locating left at the top of a reading page or a work page. Locating top is similar to finding left on the page. Some type of top marker must be seen. Many books show page numbers in the upper corners of the pages. As each page is turned, the eyes see the new page number in the top left corner. Of course, the eyes also see another page number in the top right corner of the opposite page. Persons with visual dyslexia can never be fully sure where they are just be seeing page numbers. If a moment of reversal occurs while the eyes scan the new pages, the reader who is dyslexic is forced to stop and relocate the top left markers before continuing the task. Instructors must spend time with each dyslexic student working out the best top left marker system. It will be possible to develop a visual reminder system that works most of the time.

Left-to-Right Processing

Once the learner who is dyslexic has found top left on the page, the next task is to remember to keep working left to right. Without warning the learner with visual dyslexia experiences moments of scrambled sequence. Mental images suddenly become jumbled. This is often called "static" because these interruptions are much like static that interrupts a television picture or radio signal. These episodes of mental static are very brief, no longer than a quick sneeze. When they pass, the dyslexic learner must put the pieces of the mental image back together. It is like a sudden breeze scattering leaves that must be raked together again. Thus the individual who is dyslexic repeatedly faces the task of rebuilding left-to-right orientation again and again while reading, spelling, writing, or copying.

Touching the Work Space

The most efficient strategy for rebuilding and maintaining left-to-right processing is for the learner with dyslexia always to touch the work space with a finger. At the very first sight of the work page, the student must touch the starting place as the eyes find the starting place. It is essential for the finger and the eyes to work together as a team in establishing left top orientation. Then the sense of touch continues to guide the visual channel as the learner with dyslexia proceeds left to right across the page. In writing across the page, the pencil or pen becomes the source of touch to coordinate left-to-right progress. When the dyslexic learner looks away, the sense of touch brings the eyes back to the correct place to continue writing.

Whispering While Working

It is impossible for learners who are dyslexic to work in silence. Successful persons who have dyslexia have developed a variety of whisper techniques that are vital in holding mental images together. Whispering to oneself is the glue that holds the pieces of the mental image together. Students who are severely dyslexic (level 8, 9, or 10 on the severity scale) must follow a multisensory technique in which four sensory pathways are blended at the same time. These struggling learners must see/say/hear/touch simultaneously. As the eyes see, the voice must whisper while the ears hear and fingers touch. Otherwise, mental images fall apart and the dyslexic learner is left with scrambled perceptions that do not make sense. Those who struggle hard with language processing need to say their work aloud. They must talk to themselves to hold mental images together. As literacy skills improve, this talking can be reduced to a whisper, although dyslexic whisperers will always have moments of blurting out words or thoughts when inner frustration reaches high levels. More confident learners who are dyslexic eventually learn to talk to themselves silently without any outward appearance of doing so. Their lips move slightly, revealing the inner voice activity that must occur if they are to succeed in reading and writing.

Having Enough Time

An unavoidable component of visual dyslexia is slow processing. Too many bridges are out within the "information highways" to let these learners work rapidly. As a rule, most students who are dyslexic must have double or triple the usual time to do the same amount of reading or writing. Those who are severely dyslexic (level 8 or 9 on the severity scale) often require four to five times longer than usual. Instructors must remember why these students work so slowly. The cliche "two steps forward, one step back" is the rule for those who are dyslexic. In fact, many who are dyslexic plod forward even more slowly: one step forward, two steps back. All reading, writing, spelling, and copying tasks present dyslexic learners with a constantly changing landscape. Details do not stay the same. Symbols continually reverse, change position, or appear in different sequences. Where to go next changes as left becomes right and top becomes bottom. To stay in control of this bewildering literacy landscape, persons who are dyslexic take one timid step forward, rehearse the process of finding the correct orientation, talk it over with themselves, then often lose this awareness and are forced to do it again. Meanwhile, classmates and instructors have moved ahead, leaving the struggling learner behind. The only way dyslexic learners can succeed is to have all the time they need to labor through this slow perceptual processing at their own rate. This slow processing speed cannot be hurried without creating overwhelming frustration and sense of failure.

Books on Tape

Persons with visual dyslexia often learn well through listening with excellent memory for oral information. This skill in absorbing knowledge through listening enables these students to benefit from tape-recorded reading materials. The major source for educational materials on tape is Recording for the Blind and Dyslexic (RFB&D).* When dyslexia has been diagnosed by an authorized professional, instructors can borrow a broad range of textbooks on tape. One of the goals of all local literacy programs should be to accumulate a tape library that includes all materials the instructor would like to use with struggling readers. By taping news articles, lessons from workbooks, instructions for doing assignments, and interesting short stories, instructors can build a tape library to help learners who are dyslexic compensate for poor reading skills.

ONE-ON-ONE INSTRUCTION

Instructors face enormous challenges in teaching learners who are dyslexic. It is rarely possible for these struggling students to thrive in typical classroom situations. Their learning needs are too different to let them fit into group learning. So long as dyslexic patterns remain at the severe level, it is virtually impossible for persons with dyslexia to benefit from group instruction beyond a limited level. With this in mind, instructors are challenged to provide certain types of accommodations for students who are dyslexic.

Learners with dyslexia require one-on-one instruction when new skills are presented. Even when several dyslexic students are in the same group, they cannot cope well enough with group distractions and the emotions of school failure to absorb new skill information. These learners are overly sensitive about lifelong failure. They are acutely self-conscious about appearing "dumb." They freeze up and feel immobilized in the presence

*RFB&D (20 Roszel Road, Princeton, NJ 20542; (609) 452-0606; (800) 221-4792) is a national nonprofit organization that provides taped educational books free on loan, books on diskette, library services, and other educational and professional resources to individuals who cannot read standard print because of a visual, physical, or perceptual disability.

of others when learning deficits are exposed in public. These intelligent struggling learners require one-on-one attention while they go through the labored multisensory process described above. Only in a sheltered one-on-one relationship with a patient partner can dyslexic learners feel safe enough to see it/say it/hear it/touch it to their satisfaction without feeling ashamed.

Study Partners

The most effective teaching arrangement for learners with dyslexia is to find study partners who have the time and patient temperament to guide these strugglers at their own pace. It is usually possible to recruit study partners if the literacy program is at all flexible. In fact, literacy programs like the Laubach Literacy Association and Literacy Volunteers of America are structured around the one-on-one study partner concept. A study partner need not be a certified educator. Dyslexic learners need someone who is first of all patient and nonjudgmental. The study partner should be a person who knows how to wait while the dyslexic learner takes one step forward, then two steps back. The role of the study partner is to be a helper who quietly teaches the learner who is dyslexic how to follow the markers in finding the place and working left to right through the task. The study partner is a sounding board, giving feedback when the student stumbles or becomes unsure. The study partner is a good listener, following the vocal lines coming from the learner. The study partner watches closely for those dyslexic cycles when the mental image scrambles and the pieces fall apart. Then the study partner patiently helps the student back up and put the pieces together again. The role of the study partner is to encourage, show the way, absorb frustration, and share the student's disappointment, but not to criticize. The study partner is the bridge between the classroom and the individual learner.

CHAPTER 6

Auditory Dyslexia

In Chapter 1 I reviewed the history of research of the central nervous system that discovered what causes dyslexia. It is clear that many neuronal bridges are missing and too many extra nerve pathways exist in those who are dyslexic. In Chapter 2 I presented the brain research of Livingstone et al. (1991) and Lehmkuhle et al. (1993) who discovered the missing links in the magno cells between the retina and visual cortex. These structural deficits within the visual perception highway create Irlen syndrome and other types of faulty visual perception in reading. In 1993 Paula Tallal et al. at Rutgers University reported similar gaps and missing links inside the auditory perception systems of certain individuals (cited by Blakeslee, 1994). This discovery provides evidence that a type of learning disability called *auditory dyslexia* is related to differences in brain structure.

Figure 6.1 shows the regions of the left brain where human speech is heard and interpreted. In order to understand human language, a listener must quickly comprehend the many combinations of rapid and slow chunks (phonemes) that create human speech. When an individual says and hears words, he or she actually is saying and hearing clusters of speech chunks. Some are spoken and heard very quickly. Others are spoken and heard more slowly. For example, the word cat is made of three fast/slow/fast chunks. First comes the rapid harsh sound /k/. Then comes the slower soft sound of short /a/. Finally comes the rapid hard sound /t/. Tallal's research has discovered a missing link in the left brain nerve structure where human

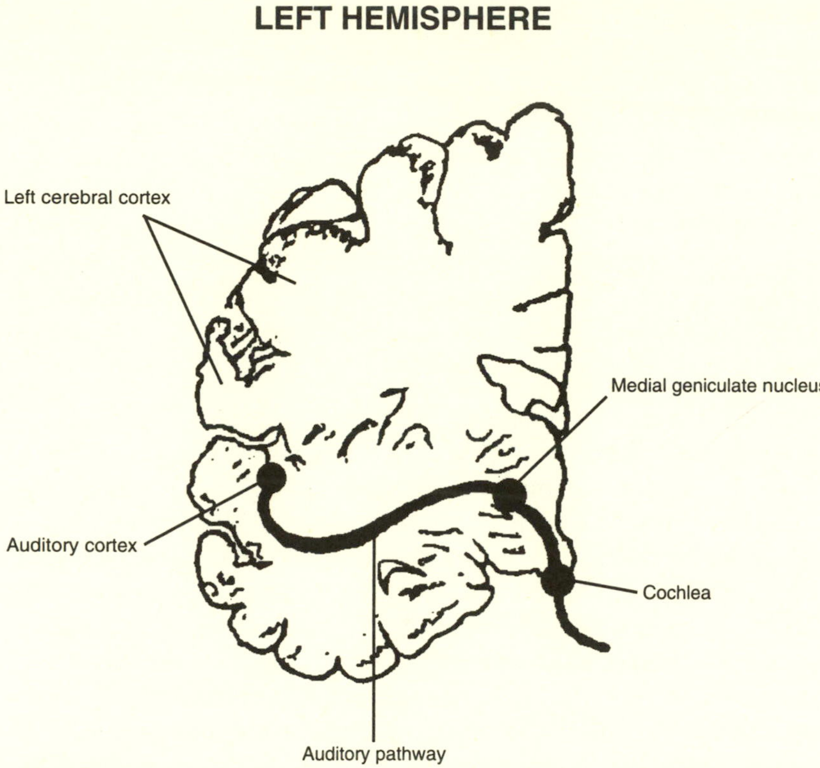

Figure 6.1. A cross section of the left brain shows the auditory pathway between the ears and the auditory cortex where sound is interpreted. Tallal et al. (1993) has shown that two types of cells transfer sound patterns from the cochlea (inner ear) through the medial geniculate nucleus to the auditory cortex. Some of these cells send chunks of sound rapidly. Other cells send sound particles more slowly. The auditory cortex assembles these fast/slow particles into complete auditory images. When the fast processing cells are underdeveloped, the person fails to hear all of the fast/slow particle patterns. This produces a "tone deaf" handicap called auditory dyslexia.

speech is processed. Persons who have auditory dyslexia are "tone deaf" to sequences of fast/slow/fast sounds. The auditory cortex does not receive complete word patterns.

The person with auditory dyslexia lives his or her life perceiving only bits and pieces of the spoken language. For these individuals, listening to human speech is like listening to a radio broadcast through thick layers of static. Parts of the oral message are heard, but important chunks of the oral flow are missing. The listener with auditory dyslexia is left to guess at what everyone else comprehends on schedule. This new knowledge confirms what many researchers have suspected for more than 100 years. Within the brain structure of approximately 10% of the human population are small but critical differences that get in the way of becoming fluent in one's native language (Jordan 1988, 1989). Auditory dyslexia creates several kinds of blocks in processing language.

POOR LISTENING

One of the first signs of auditory dyslexia is poor listening. This symptom involves much more than not paying attention. The person with auditory dyslexia tries hard to listen as others speak. But no matter how hard the person tries, he or she never absorbs the full message. As a rule, individuals with auditory dyslexia comprehend less than half of the oral information they hear the first time. If no one repeats, these listeners leave the situation with only part of the message they heard others say.

NEED TO HEAR AGAIN

Those who have auditory dyslexia usually give out signals that they need to hear it again. Instructors have no trouble spotting this need as dyslexic listeners interrupt by saying: "What? What do you mean? I didn't understand. Can you say it again?" This request to hear again is a chronic pattern. These struggling listeners continually raise a hand during lectures, asking for things to be repeated. They cannot keep up in dictation, such as writing spelling words or taking notes. They continually signal that they are lost and need the speaker to repeat. Persons who are at the severe range of auditory dyslexia (level 8, 9, or 10 on the severity scale) cannot listen without interrupting: "Huh? What? What do you mean?"

CONTINUAL MISUNDERSTANDING

The most critical hazard for those with auditory dyslexia is misunderstanding or misinterpreting what they hear. A listener who is dyslexic rarely absorbs more than half of the meaning the first time oral information is heard. This low level of listening comprehension guarantees chronic difficulty with short-term and long-term memory. If a person fails to comprehend half of what is heard, the result is chronic misunderstanding of what teachers say, what job supervisors tell, what friends confide, and what family members talk about. Phone conversations are misconstrued. News programs are misinterpreted. What one overhears others say is misunderstood. Those who have auditory dyslexia stumble through school misunderstanding and failing to comprehend much of what they hear in the classroom. When tests are given, this incomplete or misinterpreted knowledge appears as wrong answers and low scores.

DYSLEXIC SPEECH

It is not difficult to observe auditory dyslexia by listening for certain kinds of speech patterns. During childhood, youngsters with auditory dyslexia cannot fully understand what they hear others say. As these youngsters try to copy or mimic their native language, they cannot reproduce the same patterns they hear all around them. An earmark of auditory dyslexia is the tendency to say sounds and syllables out of sequence. Sometimes whole word patterns are said backwards. For example, a child with auditory dyslexia might say: "My tie is unshoeing." On a shopping trip a dyslexic youngster might ask to buy "new stringshoes for my sneakers." An excited child with auditory dyslexia might shout: "I hear a truck fire coming!" Children who grow up dyslexic seldom hear differences in similar words like furnace/thermos and leash/lease. For them the furnace in the basement is the same as the bottle that holds hot coffee. Such a listener might hear "You need to get a new lease on life," but develop the mental image of someone being led on a leash. Adults who are dyslexic often mix sounds while saying familiar words. On the television program *All in the Family*, Archie Bunker continually twisted words. He complained about Edith going to see her "groinucologist." He fussed about "the Reverend Flecher" (Felcher). A dyslexic person might say: "Joe, you left your bath tallow on the floor again." Another characteristic of dyslexia is to confuse the words ideal and idea: "I've got a great ideal about how to do that job better." We can easily hear auditory dyslexia in these kinds of speech differences that reveal the invisible deficit of hearing speech sounds incorrectly in the wrong sequence.

POOR SPELLING

Auditory dyslexia is readily seen in the person's attempt to write and spell from memory. Figure 6.2 shows examples of auditory dyslexia in a dictated spelling test. It is easy to see "tone deaf" patterns that show where the person failed to hear sounds within words. Classic signs of auditory dyslexia appear in reversed patterns inside words that contain vowel/r patterns: brid for bird; bran for barn; gril for girl. Play might be written paly. From is often written form. Figure 6.3 shows auditory dyslexia in original writing when the student had nothing from which to copy. This illustrates the chronic problem these learners face in processing long strings of words. Figure 6.4 reveals auditory dyslexia when a learner tries to take notes from lectures or write from dictation. This example reveals the depth of struggle most persons with auditory dyslexia face when they try to increase basic literacy skills.

Figure 6.5 illustrates how auditory dyslexia emerges when a dyslexic person tries to write the days of the week and months of the year. The peculiar spellings reveal gaps in hearing all the

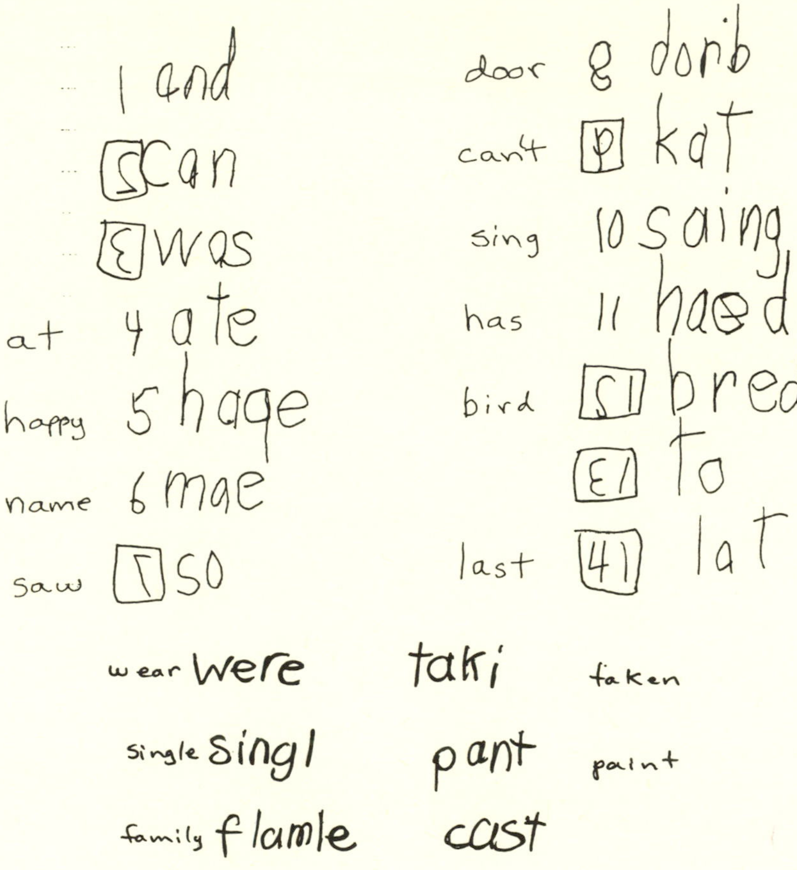

Figure 6.2. Auditory dyslexia is clearly seen in the "tone deaf" responses to spoken words. These persons cannot hear all of the fast/slow/fast speech particles as they listen to spoken words. The first student also reverses many letters and numbers while writing.

fast/slow sounds described in Tallal's research. This deficit in hearing fast/slow/fast patterns is further seen in the struggle to write the months of the year. The difference between careless spelling and dyslexic spelling is not difficult to see. Careless spelling means a mistake now and then. Dyslexic spelling

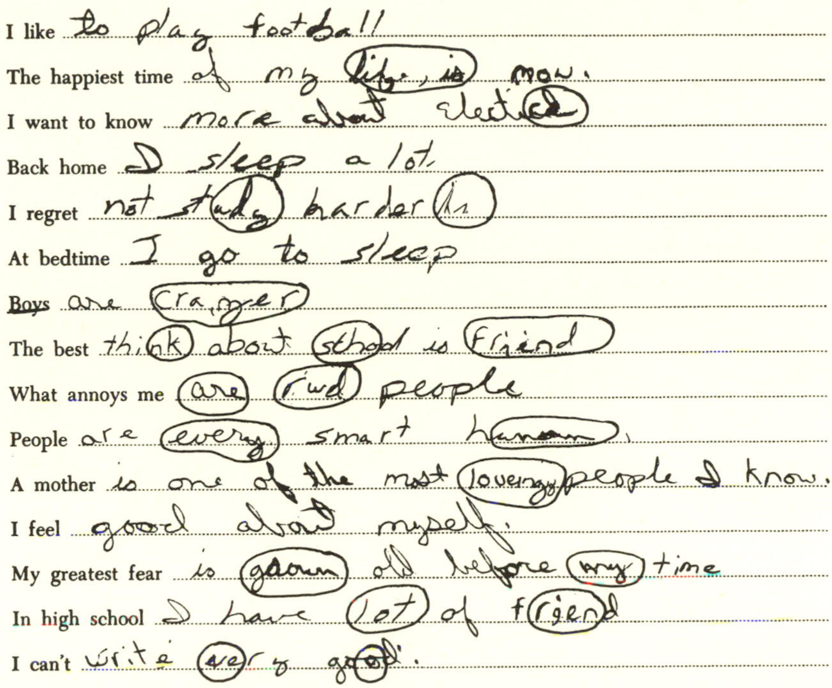
I like to play football
The happiest time of my life, is now.
I want to know more about electric
Back home I sleep a lot.
I regret not study harder
At bedtime I go to sleep
Boys are crazer
The best think about school is friend
What annoys me are rwd people
People are every smart human.
A mother is one of the most loveingy people I know.
I feel good about myself.
My greatest fear is gown old before any time
In high school I have lot of friend
I can't write very good.

Figure 6.3. This effort to write spontaneously with nothing to copy illustrates the dyslexic inability to hear all of the fast/slow sound particles in spoken language.

means chronic, constant inability to match sounds to letters, then put those patterns onto paper from memory.

SOCIAL CONFLICT

The major social consequence of auditory dyslexia is conflict. Children who begin their lives unable to hear language accurately are continually criticized, teased, and scolded for their constant language mistakes. These youngsters strike back to some degree in defending themselves against critics and tormentors. When children with dyslexia enter formal school years, their struggle with language processing becomes apparent for

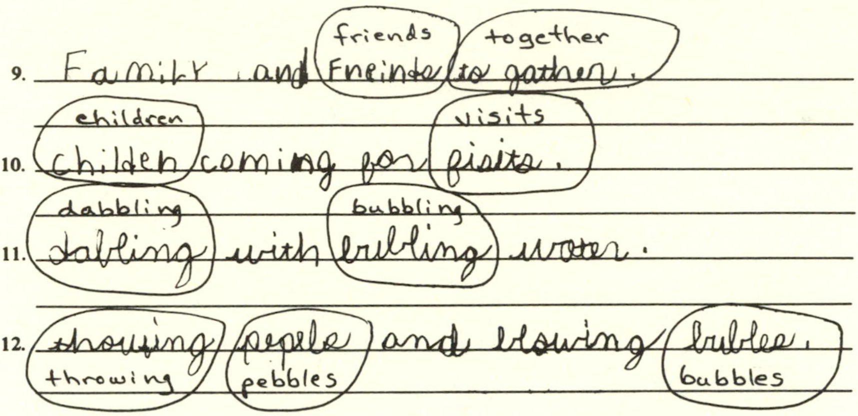

Figure 6.4. This struggle to write from dictation shows the handicapping effect of auditory dyslexia. There are too many gaps in the person's ability to hear the fast/slow sound particles.

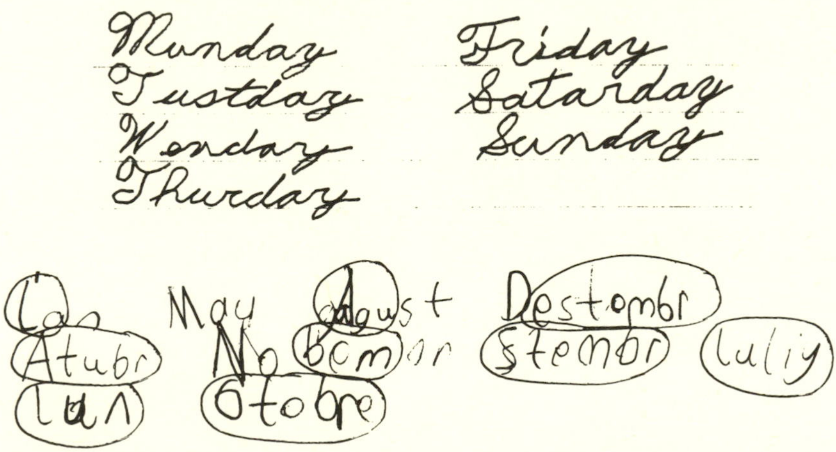

Figure 6.5. Auditory dyslexia immediately comes to the surface as the person writes the days of the weeks and months of the year.

everyone to see. Classmates, playmates, relatives, coaches, and teachers become irritated when learners with auditory dyslexia clamor to hear it again. Adolescent years are filled with frustration and humiliation as dyslexic learners lag further behind in language skills. Emerging into adulthood with humiliating patterns of auditory dyslexia guarantees conflict in most areas of the person's life. Instructors of adults with dyslexia see much social conflict as these sensitive strugglers enter yet another learning situation that holds threat of failure for them. Adults who are LD are often too quick to lash out at anyone they perceive to be a critic. They get their feelings hurt over misunderstood comments. They flare into defensive anger over what they misperceive to be insulting remarks. Instructors must deal patiently with the overflow of social conflict that usually accompanies lifelong auditory dyslexia.

CHAPTER 7

How to Compensate for Auditory Dyslexia

Before effective compensation strategies can be developed for learners with auditory dyslexia, the instructor must take time to pinpoint specific stumbling blocks that frustrate learning. The following checklist of auditory dyslexic patterns will focus the instructor's attention on certain deficits that are beyond the student's control.

AUDITORY DYSLEXIA CHECKLIST

- *Poor listening.* Does not get the full oral message. Does not remember all that was heard.
- *Needs to hear again.* Frequently says: "Huh? What? What do you mean? Could you say it again? I didn't understand."
- *Poor word pronunciation.* Continually twists sounds on the tongue. Mispronounces familiar words. Scrambles the sequence of sounds inside words. Cannot repeat words accurately.
- *Tone deaf to phonics.* Cannot hear vowel sounds or soft consonants inside words. Struggles over syllables. Cannot apply rules of phonics.
- *Very poor spelling.* Cannot remember correct spellings. Writes words the way he or she says them. Reverses inside parts of words. Leaves out word chunks while writing.
- *Gets lost taking notes.* Cannot keep up in note taking. Cannot write correctly from dictation.
- *Major struggle with writing.* Intense frustration and impa-

tience while writing. Writes very slowly with much erasing and changing.

- *Must whisper while writing.* Whispers or talks to self while writing. Rehearses spelling out loud or in a whisper. Hums while writing as he or she tries to remember.
- *Has trouble with rhyming.* Does not hear rhyming sounds. Cannot tell when words rhyme. Cannot repeat rhymes.

If a student receives one or two checks on this checklist, he or she may have mild or moderate hearing loss instead of being dyslexic. Mildy dyslexic persons who score 1 or 2 on this checklist have compensated adequately all their lives. A mild level of auditory dyslexia does not keep an intelligent person from doing well in school learning.

If a student receives 3, 4, or 5 checks on this checklist, he or she has moderate auditory dyslexia. This person may have been a successful student by receiving extra time along with help doing written projects. This individual has chronic struggle with spelling, writing, word sounding in reading, learning phonics, and pronouncing words correctly. He or she cannot hurry in academic work that involves reading, spelling, taking notes, and writing.

If a student receives 6 or more checks on this checklist, he or she has severe auditory dyslexia. A score of 6 or higher places this person at very high risk of failure in classroom learning. This individual absorbs less than half of what others say. Spelling is extremely poor. Speech is filled with tongue twists and mispronunciations. Writing is slow with frequent erasing and changing. This person cannot take notes in class, write down oral instructions or oral information on the job, fill out application forms without help, write letters without help, or do classroom writing tasks without assistance.

STRATEGIES THAT HELP AUDITORY DYSLEXIA

Learners who score 5 or higher on the auditory dyslexia checklist must have certain types of compensation to succeed in classroom learning.

Ample Time

In Chapter 5 it was explained why students who are dyslexic must have extra time. There are too many differences in brain pathway structures to let dyslexic learners hurry. This need for extra time is critical for those who have auditory dyslexia. The struggle to absorb a flow of new oral information becomes overwhelming if the dyslexic listener is pressed to hurry. Persons with dyslexia who score 5 or higher on the checklist need as much as three times longer to process information. Instructors can determine how much extra time each student needs by observing how much work can be finished in a given amount of time. Once that rate of processing is discovered, all assignments must be tailored to fit the individual's speed of thinking.

Reduced Quantities of Required Work

Instructors must keep in mind the critical factor of fatigue in learners who are LD. It is difficult for persons who are not LD to appreciate how much mental and emotional energy must be expended for struggling learners to succeed. Tasks that are easily and quickly done by most students loom like dreaded mountains for LD strugglers. For a dyslexic person to turn out acceptable written work, he or she must maintain intense concentration, stay in control of panic surges, tune out distractions, and call on enormous amounts of self-discipline. Learners who are dyslexic face the constant threat of rapid burnout that leaves them exhausted, discouraged, fearful, and even angry. Once an LD struggler reaches burnout, he or she can no longer function effectively. Work quotas must be tailored to fit each student's tolerance for stress.

Help with Listening

Chapter 5 reviewed the need for study partners to provide feedback as learners who are LD work through assigments.

Those with auditory dyslexia must have a similar kind of compensatory help with listening. Important oral information must be reviewed to make sure that all listening gaps are filled in. Listening partners spend a few minutes during break times, study times, and after class repeating oral instructions and summarizing important oral information one on one with the dyslexic listener.

Visual Summaries

Learners who have auditory dyslexia must see outlines of what they are expected to absorb through listening. These strugglers learn best when instructors write outlines, important phrases, and vocabulary words on the chalkboard. Instructors should follow printed outlines of lectures that let dyslexic students see as they hear. Homework assignments are jotted on stickers attached to book pages showing which pages are to be studied before the next class.

Visual Phonics

Students with auditory dyslexia cannot hear many of the sound units (phonemes) that make up oral and written words. These learners have to see phonetic patterns, not try to hear them. Instructors must not press these struggling learners to hear phonics. Persons who are dyslexic must see chunks inside words, mark those chunks with visual signals that remind what the symbols say, then whisper and touch until the correct sounds are connected to the printed patterns.

Learners with dyslexia seldom have trouble remembering which letters are vowels and which are consonants. This foundation knowledge must be learned first. Before any effort is made to teach phonics, instructors should guide learners who are dyslexic in connecting correct names to each alphabet letter: "aye" for a, "bee" for b, "see" for c, and so forth. As this sight recognition and naming of letters is done, students practice locating vowels and consonants by seeing and counting them, not by hearing them.

The most effective way to teach visual phonics to struggling learners is to use a multisensory approach. The student looks for (sees) specific vowel or consonant patterns. The student touches those printed patterns with a finger or marks them with a pencil. Then the student practices connecting the correct sound to those patterns by saying and hearing each sound. This four-way process (see/say/hear/touch) usually enables a learner with auditory dyslexia to work out phonetic patterns while reading or analyzing words.

Marking Vowels

Since the earliest days of literacy instruction, beginning readers have been taught phonics by drawing marks above vowel letters. Vowels that say long sounds are marked by a *macron* (ā). Vowels that say short sounds are marked by a *breve* (ŏ). This simple system of visual phonics is the most effective way to teach dyslexic students to decode phonetic patterns as they read. Because they cannot hear softer vowel and consonant sounds within words, these learners seldom comprehend traditional rules of phonics. Instead, students who are dyslexic learn to see phonetic chunks, then mark them as part of a multisensory word sounding process. The following simple guidelines of seeing and marking help dyslexic learners connect sounds to letters correctly.

One vowel.

When one vowel is alone inside a short word, it usually says its short name: măn jĕt bĭt hŏt bŭt gy̆m.

When one vowel is alone at the start of a short word, it usually says its short name: ăt ĕnd ĭt ŏf ŭp.

When one vowel is alone at the end of a short word, it usually says its long name: wē Hī sō mȳ.

Two vowels together.

When two vowels come together in a short word, the first vowel usually says its long name and the other vowel says nothing: ēa̸t māi̸n bēa̸t sōa̸p Sūe̸ sēe̸.

Sometimes both vowels speak: Bu ick ri ot.

Vowel families.

When certain vowels are together, they create special family names. These vowel families do not have markers.

aw	ew	ou	ou	ow	ow
saw	few	out	you	low	bow

Two vowels not together.

When two vowels are in a short word, but the vowels are not together, the first one usually says its long name and the second one says nothing: āte̸ sāme̸ Pēte̸ rīde̸ hōpe̸ mūle̸ ty̅pe̸.

Vowels followed by r.

When r comes after one or two vowels, a special sound is created: car her year sir door soar your fur

Exceptions to these rules.

Many familiar words do not follow these basic rules of phonics. Learners who are LD must develop pocket lists of words that break these rules. Instructors and tutors should help dyslexic students develop lists of exceptions, such as the following:

to	too	bread	weigh	you	mother
do	poor	steak	height	would	bother
who	tool	tear		sour	
	food	year		pour	

Chunking Consonants

Learners who are auditory dyslexic seldom can identify speech sounds well enough to comprehend the concept of syllables. An effective way for readers with dyslexia to break words into sound units is to use a historic method called *chin bumping*. The student places one hand below the chin while saying words slowly. Wherever the chin bumps (drops down), the word is divided or chunked. Then the student draws a slash mark between the chunks.

One consonant between two vowels.

When one consonant is between two vowels, the first vowel usually says its long name. The first chunk ends with the long vowel name where the slash mark is drawn:
rā/dar pē/can pī/lot sō/ber mō/tor rū/ler pȳ/lon.

Two consonants together inside a word.

When two consonants are together inside a word, the word usually breaks between the two consonants: bat/ter sal/sa let/ter Les/ter sit/ter mis/ter wis/dom top/ping

Three consonants together inside a word.

When three consonants are together, the word usually breaks after the first consonant:
ram/ble bat/tle sim/ple lit/tle bot/tle bub/ble puz/zle

These are examples of how visual phonics is presented to struggling learners who are auditory dyslexic. A complete visual phonics method for teaching reading to adults who are dyslexic is found in the *Jordan Prescriptive/Tutorial Reading Program* (Jordan, 1989). A manual containing many practical suggestions for teaching visual phonics is presented in *Teaching*

Adults: A Literacy Resource Book (Laubach Literacy Action, 1994).

Help with Spelling

Perhaps the greatest frustration of auditory dyslexia is lifelong poor spelling. It is seldom possible for learners who are dyslexic to develop good spelling from memory. Too many bridges are out along the "auditory highway" to let these strugglers build memory patterns for spelling. Some individuals with dyslexia can develop basic skills for functional spelling by concentrating on word families: ay ew igh or, and so forth. By substituting different consonants, families of familiar words can be memorized:

ay	ew	igh	or
day	new	high	for
way	few	might	core
say	dew	tight	more
pay	knew	sight	bore

Persons with auditory dyslexia must take a practical, functional approach to spelling. Instead of struggling to memorize hundreds of words seen in daily reading, they concentrate on specific words they must write on the job or use in keeping their lives organized. The most effective strategy for LD persons is to develop pocket lists of all the words they must spell correctly in earning a living, managing money, shopping, traveling, and so forth. New words are added only when there is enough need to have correct spellings at hand. Spellers who are dyslexic are too easily overwhelmed if the spelling list becomes too long or overly complicated.

Electronic Spelling Guides

As we approach the 21st century, adults who are dyslexic have access to a wide variety of electronic support systems designed to help with spelling. The Franklin spelling computers are an example of this kind of electronic assistance. A variety of small, portable electronic spellers are available that fit into a pocket, purse, or book bag. Several models of these electronic spelling helpers pronounce words as they appear on the screen. Some computer-based spelling systems spell words orally and pronounce the syllables. Most word processors include dictionaries that help the writer find spelling mistakes and correct them. It is possible to purchase talking computers that read back what the writer has entered into the word processor. As new types of literacy technology emerge, dyslexic adults will have many choices of electronic help with spelling.

CHAPTER 8

Dysgraphia and Dyscalculia

DYSGRAPHIA

From the early days of public education, a distinguishing hallmark of an educated person has been good penmanship. Teaching children to write neatly, legibly, and correctly has occupied countless hours of elementary school instruction. Pupils with the best penmanship have been awarded prizes and the joy of seeing their handwriting displayed on bulletin boards. To the frustration of good teachers everywhere, every class has included a few learners who could not develop good penmanship, no matter how hard they tried. Today we know why. Being dyslexic usually means that good handwriting is difficult, if not impossible. Figure 8.1 shows the fine motor control region (TCM) of the left brain where handwriting signals originate for most individuals. If the nerve pathways within the TCM are fully developed on schedule, the child builds good handwriting skills during early school years. When nerve pathways are incomplete or too many neuronal bridges are out in the fine motor control region of the left brain, the individual cannot make correct pencil motions to produce clear, neat, correct handwriting. This is called *dysgraphia*.

Dysgraphia is not a matter of carelessness in writing. If a person is a careless writer, he or she can easily correct that deficit through practice and trying harder. Being dysgraphic means that complete mental images do not pass through the fingers onto paper. Along the way between the brain and the fingertips, too many "short circuits" occur. The pen or pencil receives incomplete or partly scrambled signals, making the handwriting

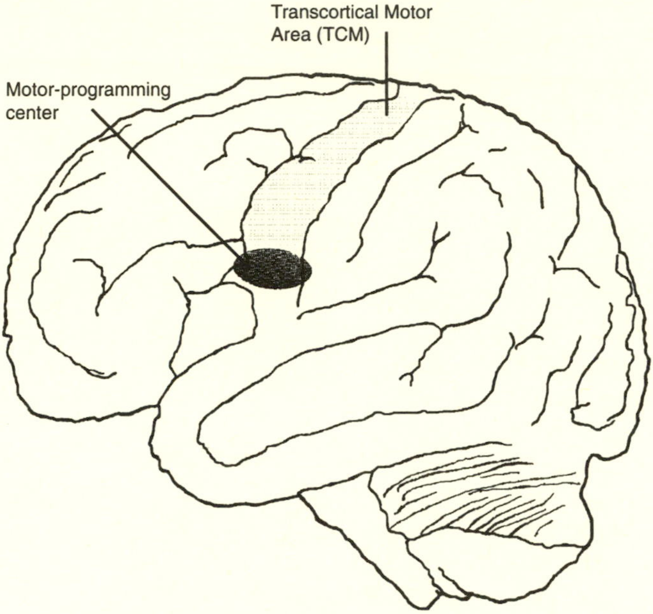

Figure 8.1. Dysgraphia originates in the motor-programming regions of the left cerebral cortex. Underdeveloped nerve pathways deliver mixed or scrambled signals to the fingers while the pencil or pen is at work. Backward strokes occur. Chunks are left out of letters or numbers. Symbols are often rotated or partly turned over.

virtually impossible to decipher. Figure 8.2 shows Vince's severe dysgraphic struggle to produce legible cursive symbols in writing the alphabet from memory. If one slowly traces over his writing, one can appreciate the frustration and exasperation of this intelligent adult who is dysgraphic. By carefully tracing Vince's writing, one can feel the many points at which the pencil turned the wrong way, made an extra stroke, or could not remember which way to turn next. All his life Vince has been scolded for not trying harder to write neatly. Ironically, he has done his very best, but his best dysgraphic effort has never been good enough to satisfy school expectations.

Figure 8.3 shows Shannon's dysgraphic writing. This intelligent student is at Level 8 (severe range) in dyslexic struggle to

Figure 8.2. Vince struggled for 27 minutes to produce this dysgraphic alphabet sequence. He was so frustrated he had to rest to be able to go on with more writing.

read and spell. He has good listening skills and learns quickly by hearing oral information. Shannon has excellent oral vocabulary that permits him to mask his LD struggle by speaking fluently and intelligently. His dyslexic tendencies spring to life on any writing task he attempts. This dysgraphic writing is filled with reversed letters and numbers (g s a 5), upside down letters (d), broken letters with chunks left out, and letters partly rolled over. Pencil pressure is extremely heavy so that the writing soon becomes smudged. Without warning the pencil cuts downward through the line or floats upward above the line. Spacing between letters and words is ragged and uneven. Some symbols are bunched too close together with edges of letters or numerals touching or overlapping. Suddenly large gaps appear when the pencil moves too far before touching down for the next point of writing. Yet beneath all these dysgraphic patterns is intelligent sentence structure that reflects the good verbal skills people hear when Shannon tells instead of writes.

Figure 8.4 shows dysgraphic struggle as Wayne composed a note to his instructor. Spontaneous writing when the person has nothing to copy brings dysgraphia quickly to the surface. Figure 8.4 shows the continual scratching out, marking over, and constant erasing seen when dysgraphic writers must communicate on paper. Holes are often rubbed through the paper and the writing space is covered by eraser crumbs. Instructors

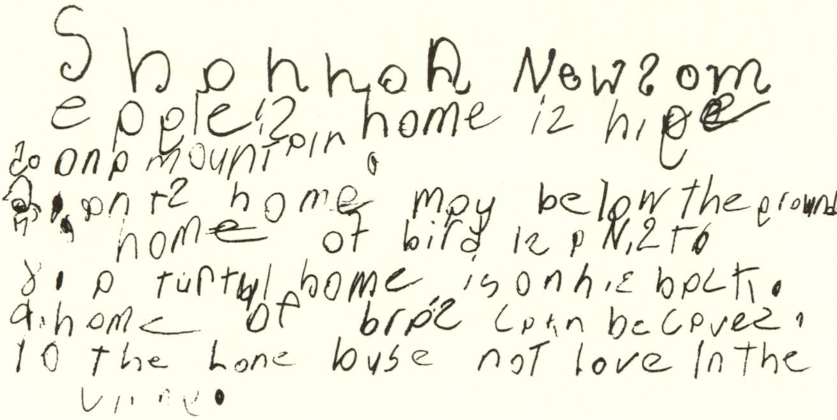

Figure 8.3. Shannon worked on this language assignment more than 30 minutes. It is possible to decipher what he wrote by noticing backward letters (g in eagle's and high), a written like p, d written like p, as well as broken letters with incomplete edges.

must remember that students like Wayne do their very best. Figure 8.4 shows the best he could do after struggling half an hour to write the note.

Figure 8.5 shows another face of dysgraphia. When persons who are dysgraphic try to draw or copy geometric shapes, the pencil often moves in the opposite direction. Dysgraphia is immediately seen when the person tries to draw or copy a diamond. As the pencil reaches the corner and must turn in a new direction, a reversed motion sends the pencil the opposite way, creating an "ear" on the corner of the diamond segment. Persons who are dysgraphic struggle all their lives to draw or copy patterns that include diamond shapes.

Figure 8.6 shows further dysgraphic struggle in copying simple geometric shapes. Learners who are dysgraphic cannot produce neat, correctly drawn patterns unless they are allowed to trace. Even in tracing the pencil struggles to stay on the line, follow curves, and turn corners correctly. Instructors must remember that none of this pencil control struggle is caused by carelessness. Dysgraphia is created by underdeveloped nerve

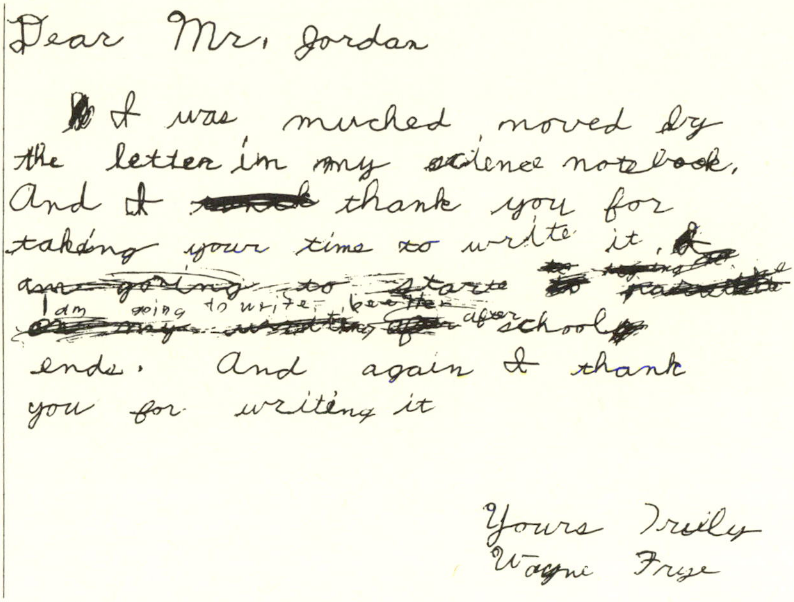
Dear Mr. Jordan

I was muched moved by the letter in my science notebook. And I thank you for taking your time to write it. I am going to write back after school ends. And again I thank you for writing it

Yours Truly
Wayne Frye

Figure 8.4. Constant dysgraphic slips of the pencil keeps Wayne in a state of intense frustration as he writes. Only his strong determination to earn his GED diploma kept him involved in a literacy upgrade program.

pathways that send incomplete or scrambled signals to the writing fingers.

DYSCALCULIA

A similar kind of encoding struggle is often seen in arithmetic. Basic arithmetic processing (adding, subtracting, multiplying, dividing) is accomplished mostly in the left brain where dyslexia usually occurs. Most learners who are dyslexic also struggle with basic arithmetic skills. It is often impossible for them to develop short-term or long-term memory for the hundreds of number facts required for accurate computation. When these struggling learners try to write number informa-

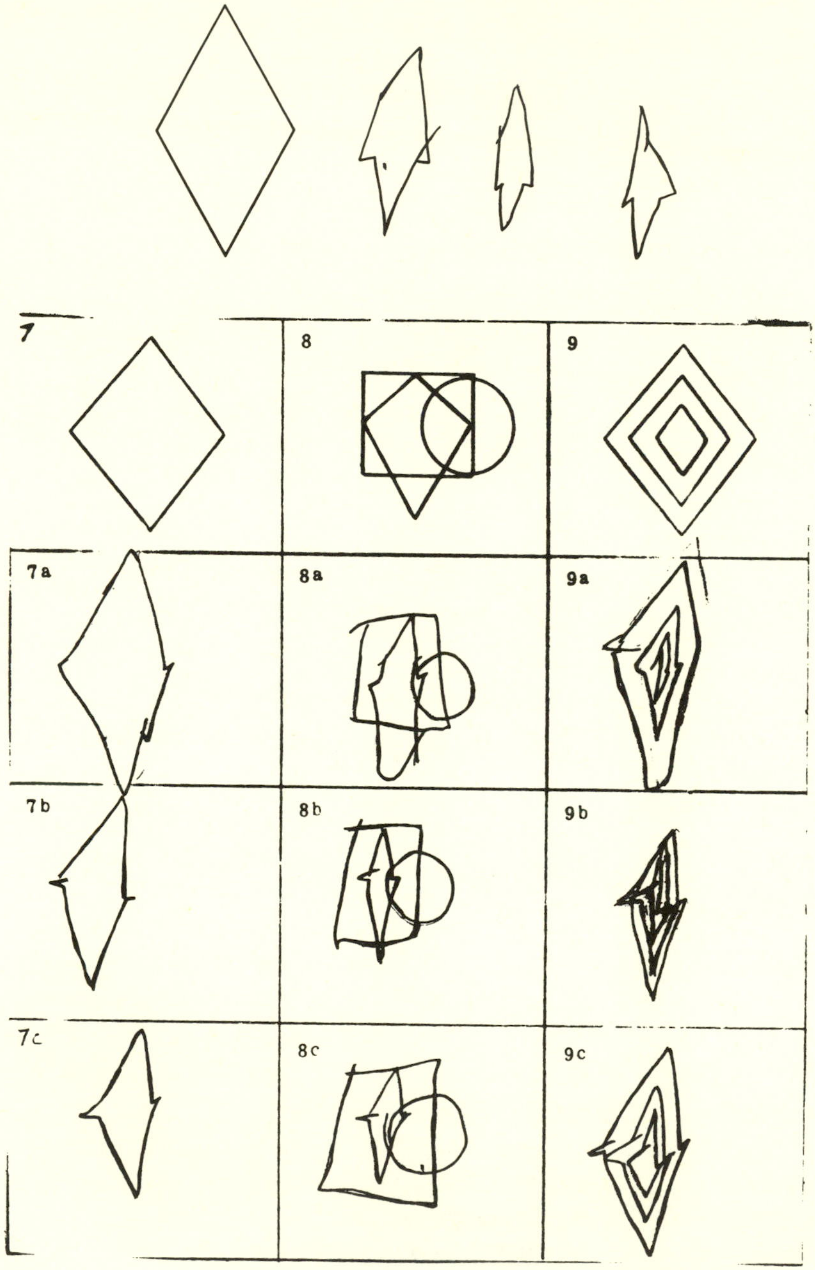

Figure 8.5. Continual dysgraphic slips of the fingers create "ears" on the corners of diamonds. When the pencil reaches the corner, the fingers inadvertently go the opposite direction.

Figure 8.6. Dysgraphia is a critical factor when standardized motor coordination tests are administered. These examples are from the *Stanford Binet Intelligence Scale, Form LM.* These bright learners lost IQ points on their test performance because of dysgraphic struggle.

tion or work arithmetic problems, they cannot maintain full mental images of all the math processes. This lifelong difficulty doing arithmetic is called *dyscalculia.*

The most obvious signs of dyscalculia occur when a struggling learner cannot do mental computation. Figure 8.7 and Figure 8.8 illustrate Brad's frustration trying to do simple arith-

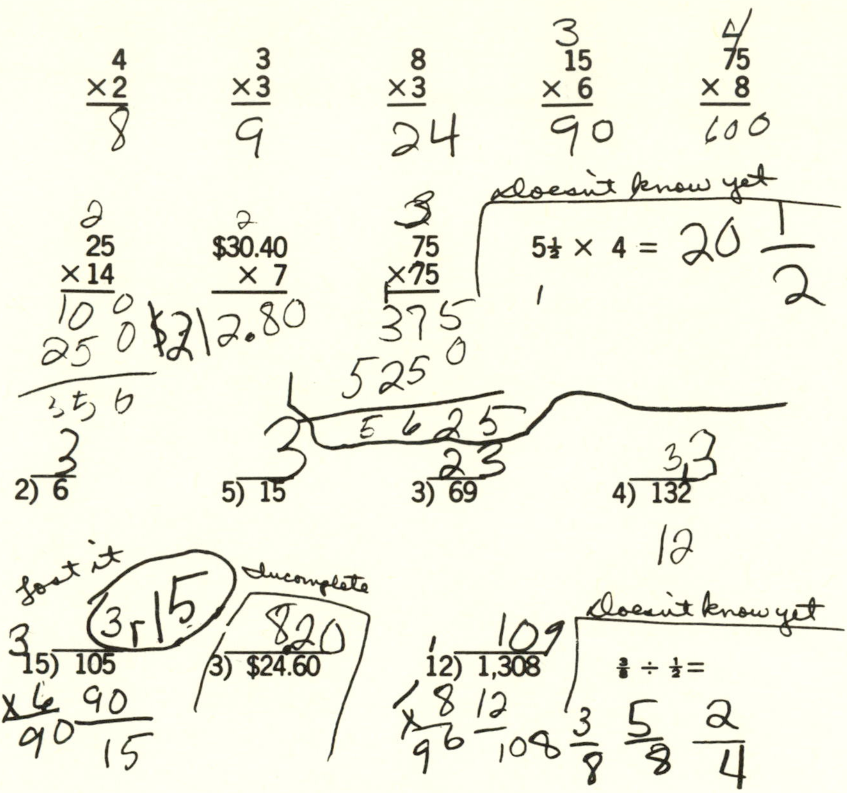

Figure 8.7. Dysgraphia frustrates Brad as he works math assignments. He cannot reduce his pencil strokes small enough to fit his writing into the work spaces on the page. All his life teachers have fussed at him for "always being so messy."

metic computation. In order to work a page of multiplication and division problems (Figure 8.7), he filled a tablet page with random figuring (Figure 8.8). Over and over he tried first one strategy by practicing on scratch paper. Then he tried another strategy while he counted fingers and talked to himself: "Let's see. I think I multiply. OK, that's going to work. Ooops! I forgot to borrow. No, that's not right. I'm supposed to carry. Damn! I did it again. OK, now let's see. Oh, yeah. I'm supposed to take the first number times the second number. . . . . . " By

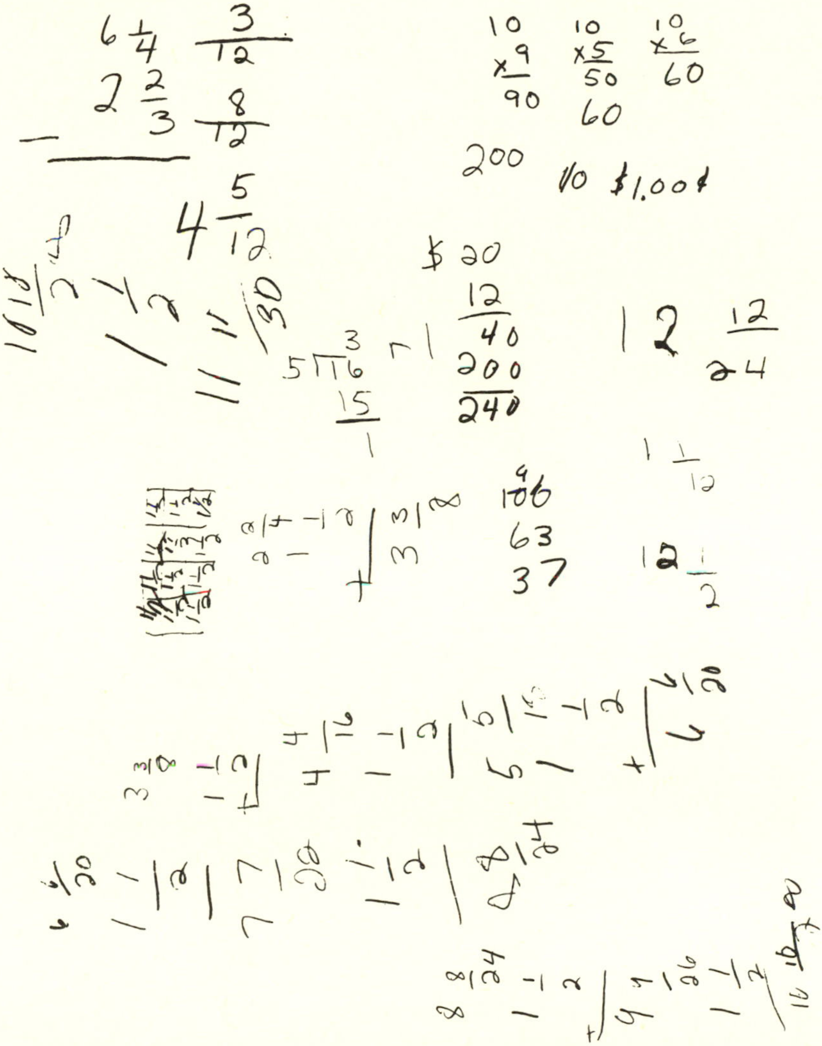

Figure 8.8. Dyscalculia also frustrates Brad. To do this simple math assignment, he had to fill a tablet page with trial-and-error practice. It is impossible for him to work arithmetic problems from memory.

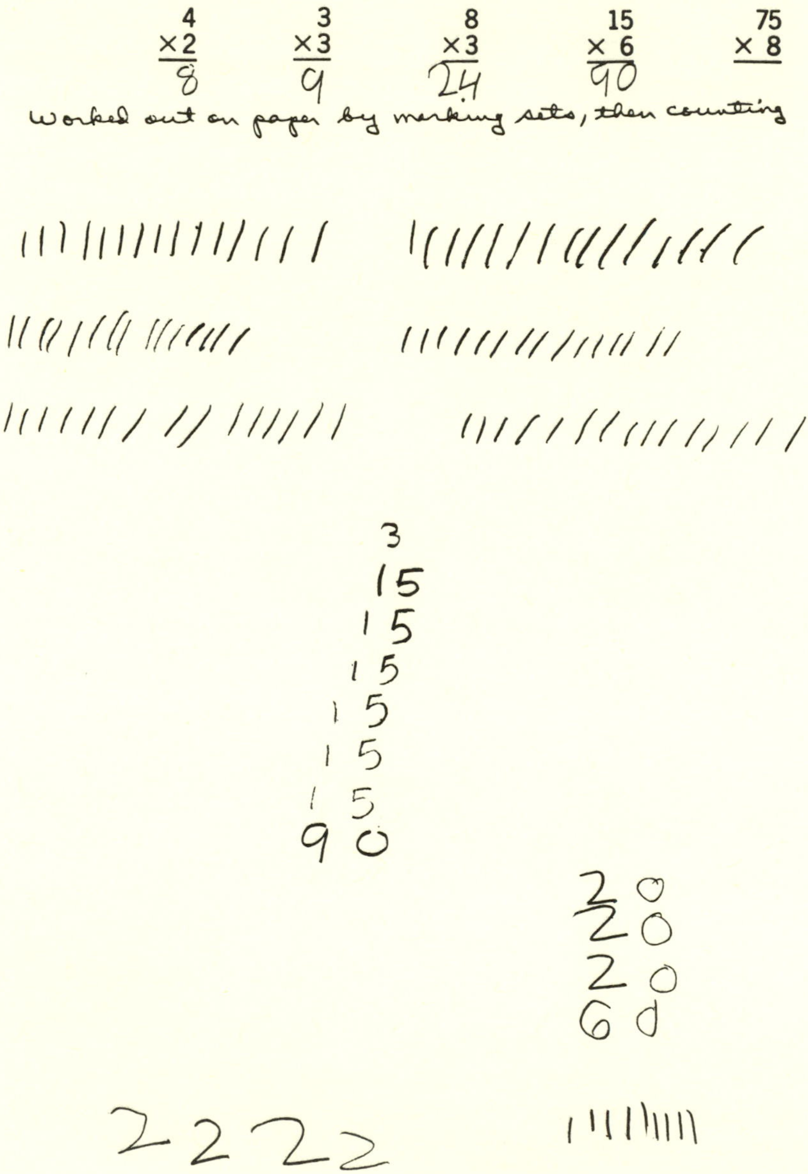

Figure 8.9. Dyscalculia also frustrates Andrea. To do this simple math assignment, she had to do trial-and-error practice on scratch paper. After 10 years of formal school experience, she still cannot do math from memory.

this time Brad was so frustrated he had to take a break. At age 35, this intelligent man cannot do simple arithmetic without this kind of paper/pencil rehearsal.

Figure 8.9 shows Andrea's work on the same arithmetic assignment that frustrated Brad so intensely (Figure 8.7). Quietly and methodically, she drew sets of lines, then counted them while whispering over and over to herself. To multiply 6 x 15, she wrote 15 six times, then added. Carefully she touched each number as she said it to herself. To find 3 x 20, she wrote 20 three times and slowly added, touching and whispering to make sure she did not lose her place. At age 42, Andrea has struggled with arithmetic all her life. In preparing for the GED test she is determined to master the basic arithmetic skills that have eluded her since childhood. Yet no matter how much she practices or how hard she tries, she cannot develop long-term memory for the basic facts of arthmetic computation. Dyscalculia forces her to return to this slow, tedious compensation technique every time she must do arithmetic.

Dyscalculia makes it impossible for learners to function with story problems that present math facts in sentences or paragraphs. As learners like Brad and Andrea read math information, the facts do not develop into an organized or sequential mental image. Learners with dyscalculia do not build mental images of arithmetic facts or math information by reading it. This form of dyslexia blocks math processing the way other forms of dyslexia block spelling and word analysis.

CHAPTER 9

How to Compensate for Dysgraphia and Dyscalculia

Perhaps the most difficult challenge for those who teach struggling learners is understanding that LD patterns cannot be cured or changed beyond a point. Adolescents and adults who are dyslexic, dysgraphic, or who have dyscalculia will never be free of these lifelong symptoms of learning disability. Chapter 4 provided an explanation of the difference between deep (primary) dyslexia and secondary (developmental) dyslexia. Children who have secondary dyslexia move down the severity scale as they advance through adolescence and into early adulthood. More than half of the original LD struggle may have disappeared by the age 25; however, these late developers will always stumble over remnants of LD. Those with more severe forms of childhood LD will carry those stumbling blocks to learning into adulthood. Remedial tutoring and countless hours of practice on basic skills often reduce the level of struggle by building partly fluent literacy skills that can be hidden beneath the surface of strong self-confidence. But adolescents and adults who still struggle with LD patterns will do so all their lives. The focus of instructors and tutors must not be to take away the underlying perceptual difficulties. The focus must be on compensating for specific language-processing deficits.

COMPENSATING FOR DYSGRAPHIA

As explained in Chapter 8, dysgraphia is caused by underdeveloped nerve pathways within the fine motor control area of the left brain. Being dysgraphic means that all written work will be extremely slow and labored. The following guidelines present the types of compensation that enable dysgraphic persons to cope with writing requirements.

Multisensory Processing

It is impossible for persons who are dysgraphic to write silently. Silent writing focuses upon only two major sensory pathways: sight and touch. In silent writing, the individual silently transfers mental images onto paper. This two-channel work style is not effective for those who are dysgraphic. In order to develop and hold complete mental images during the act of writing, persons with dysgraphia must use four sensory pathways at the same time: sight/touch/speech/hearing. They must be encouraged to whisper or murmer to themselves as they slowly write what they are thinking and saying.

Enough Time

Learners who are LD cannot hurry in processing literacy information. This need for extra time is especially critical for those who are dysgraphic. For these strugglers to transfer mental images onto paper, a great deal of extra time is required, as mentioned in Chapter 8. When dysgraphic persons try to speed up their writing, their already handcapped penmanship becomes even less legible. Instructors must plan for dysgraphic writers to have all the time they need to do their very best.

Frequent Breaks

Within a short period of time after starting to write, muscles in the fingers and hand of those who are dysgraphic begin to ache and cramp. It is essential for these strugglers to pace themselves, stopping often to shake out the cramps or rub the ache out of fingers and hands. Dysgraphic learners must be taught to recognize the first signs of muscle fatigue in fingers and hands. These individuals must learn not to push themselves to the point of fine motor burnout. Dysgraphic writers must feel free to stop every few words to relax their writing muscles. Then they can move ahead to write a few more words before stopping again. When required writing is done this way with plenty of time and frequent stops to rest, persons who are dysgraphic can produce more legible written work than they might think possible.

Double Spacing

Those who are dysgraphic must not write on every line. Figure 9.1 shows what happens when dysgraphic writers use every line. Soon it becomes impossible to read what has been written as symbols, words, and lines crowd together. Figure 9.2 and Figure 9.3 illustrate why all writing by dysgraphic learners must be double spaced. When room is left between the words and between the lines, both the student and instructor can interpret and correct what was written. Learners who are dysgraphic often need to lay a finger at the end of each word to establish enough space before writing the next word.

Visible Left Margin

Learners who are dysgraphic often do not pay attention to the subtle left margin line on tablet paper or writing paper. Figure 9.4 shows the kind of bold visual marking an instructor should use in preparing writing paper for dysgraphic learners. As writing assignments are done, students who are dysgraphic are reminded frequently to "bump the left margin" in doing columns and to "make the pencil stay on the dark line" when spacing words and writing sentences.

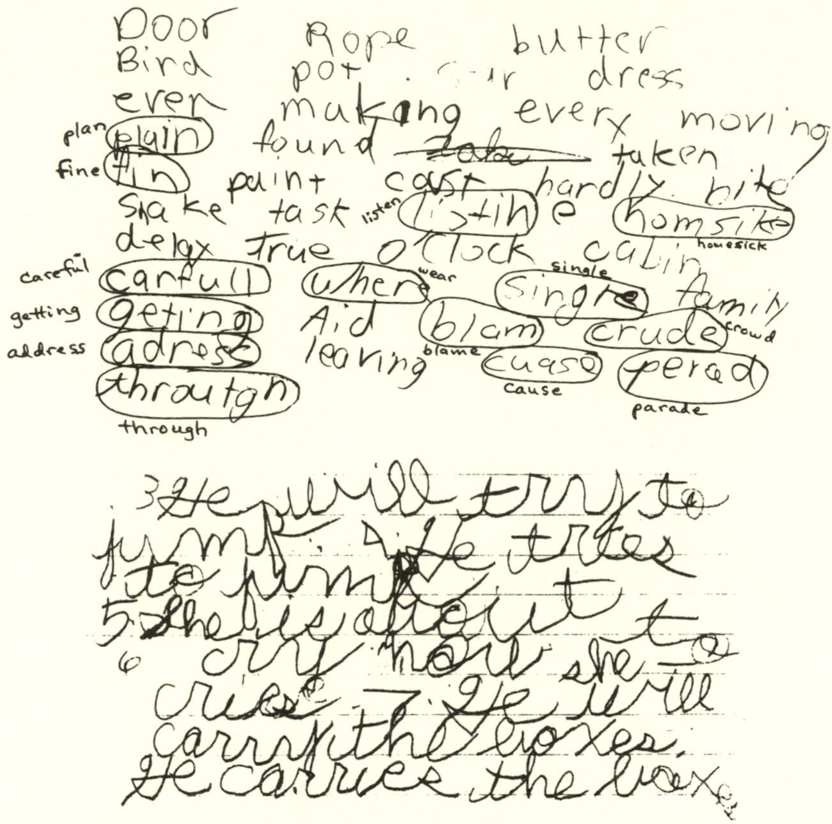

Figure 9.1. Dysgraphic writing is almost impossible to decode when it is crammed together on every line.

Reduce the Quantity

Those who teach learners who are dysgraphic must make choices when it comes to requiring written assignments and homework of struggling writers. If it is impossible for these students to produce as much writing as classmates who are not dysgraphic, then how much paper/pencil word should these students be required to do? Chapter 4 presented the rule of thumb that those who are LD need two to three times longer than usual to do their best. The necessity to find out how much

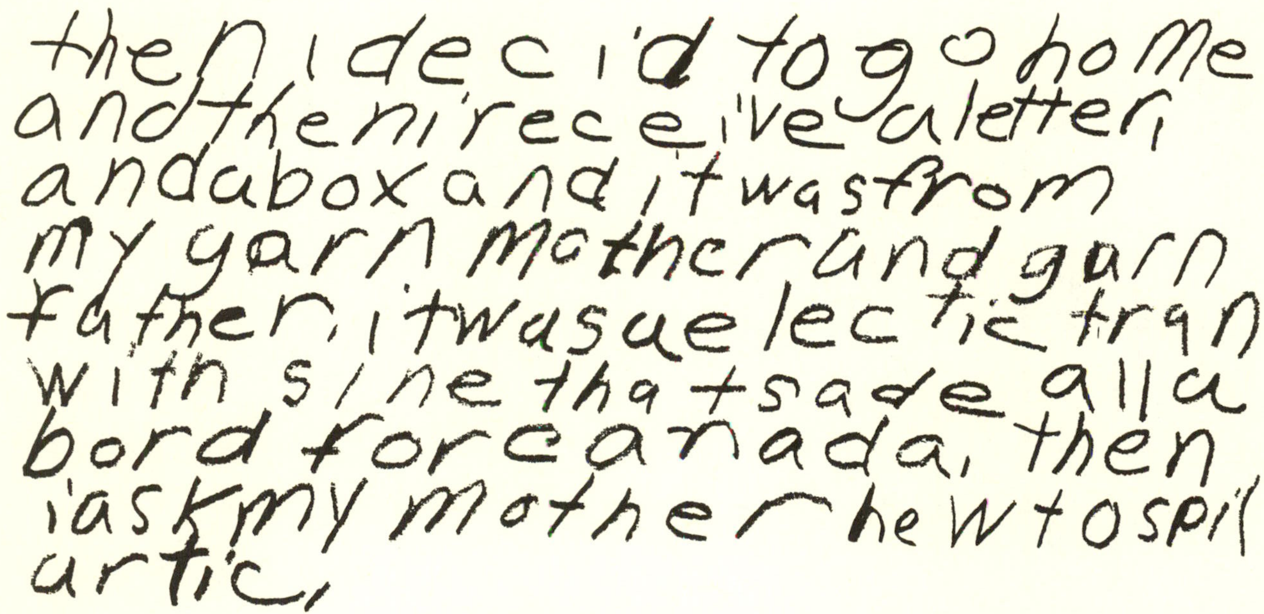

Figure 9.2. The assignment was to write a paragraph about a childhood memory related to a birthday experience. The student who produced this dysgraphic writing could not read it later. The instructor guided him in separating the words and lines (see Figure 9.3). When each word and line were spaced, it was easy to decode this story.

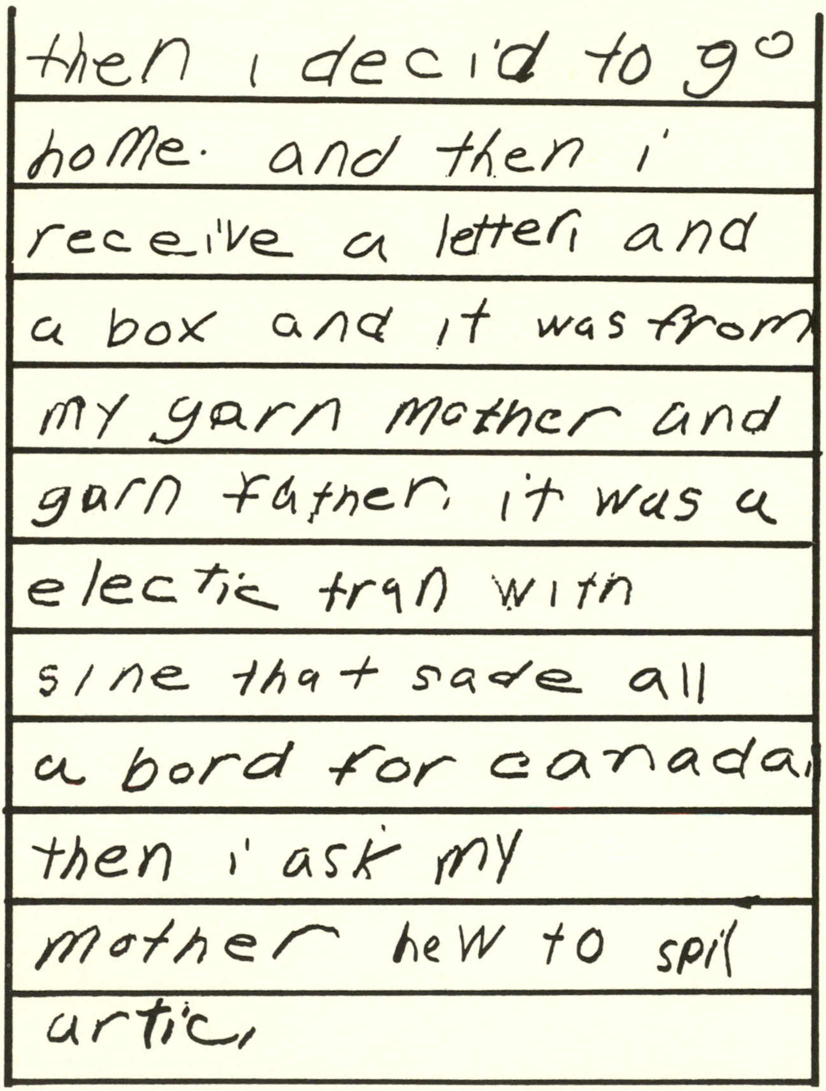

then i decid to go
home. and then i
receive a letter and
a box and it was from
my garn mother and
garn father it was a
electic tran with
sine that sade all
a bord for canada
then i ask my
mother hew to spil
artic,

Figure 9.3. Spacing between words and lines allows dysgraphic writing to be analyzed more easily. With ample space, students can improve skills in editing and self-correcting.

Figure 9.4. Work pages with bold lines and margins should be duplicated on softly colored paper, as noted in Chapter 3.

work each student can do well in a certain length of time was explained. Chapter 8 introduced three dysgraphic writers: Vince, Shannon, and Wayne. Figure 8.4 demonstrated that Wayne needed half an hour to write a simple note to his instructor. How much writing should these dysgraphic learners be required to do? Instructors face a choice: either allow enough extra time to permit the student to do the full assignment well, or else cut back on the quantity so that the task matches each student's speed of processing.

Require Legibility

When work quotas are correctly matched with the student's speed of processing, the instructor can safely require that all written assignments be done legibly. By providing well marked writing paper that spaces words and lines, and by giving plenty of time to let each student work comfortably, instructors can ask that all written work be legible. Even severely dysgraphic learners like Wayne and Shannon can produce legible writing if they are taught to compensate. Each writer who is dysgraphic chooses whether to write in manuscript print or cursive style, whichever is better for the most nearly legible writing.

Help with Editing

No dysgraphic learner should be expected to edit his or her own writing without help. All editing must be done with a partner who talks through the process of looking for errors. The editing partner must be a patient person who does not press the dysgraphic student to hurry. Oral feedback is the key to success for editing written work. As the struggling writer searches for errors (misspellings, reversed letters, upside down symbols), he or she talks it over with the editing partner. By following this multisensory strategy of seeing/saying/hearing/

touching, the writer who is dysgraphic will locate many more errors than he or she can do alone.

Dictating to a Scribe

As was clear in Chapter 8, Shannon and Wayne had intelligent things to say. Yet they could not express very much of their intelligence or ideas through handwriting. It is essential for dysgraphic learners to work part of the time with a scribe who writes what the struggling writer dictates. If a scribe is not available, LD learners like Shannon and Wayne can dictate their thoughts into a tape recorder. Self-confident students who are dysgraphic often enjoy making videotapes by speaking to a camera. Being free to express themselves orally instead of through handwriting is a liberating experience for most persons who struggle with penmanship. Before a story or report is dictated, instructors work with the dysgraphic person preparing an outline of what is to be expressed orally. The main ideas are planned ahead. Then the student is free to fill in the outline orally with none of the restrictions encountered so quickly in writing.

Semantic Mapping

Figure 9.5 shows a highly effective strategy that guides LD learners in organizing their ideas before they start to write. The main idea is written in the middle of the page (My Job). Then the student jots down ideas as they come to mind. At first, these notes may seem random: 9 hours a day overtime $7.85 an hour 4 years don't like boss want new job too boring. After the student has finished making his or her notes on the map, a study partner helps the person put these ideas together into a paragraph or a story. Writers who are dysgraphic can dictate to a scribe as the pieces are assembled into an organized form. By lumping ideas inside circles, this mapping strategy is

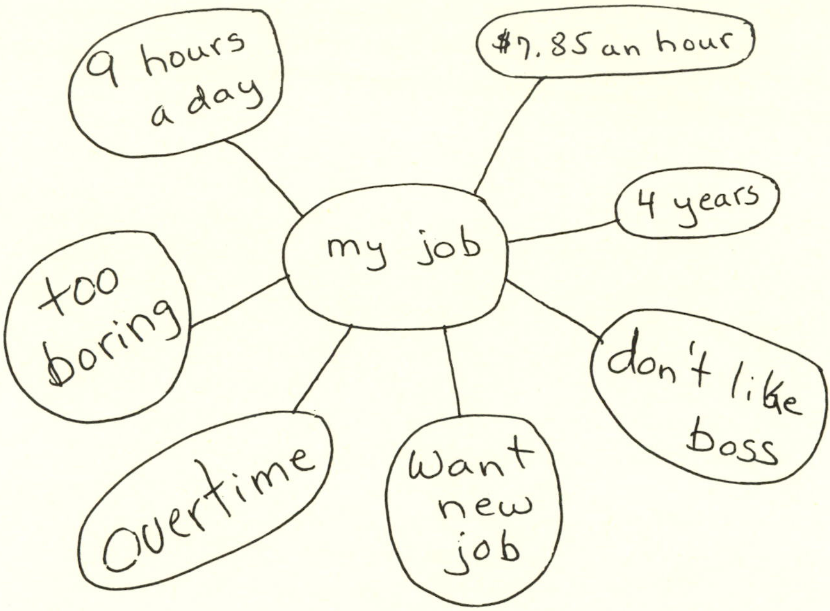

Figure 9.5. Semantic mapping is a highly effective way to help learners who are dyslexic organize their ideas before they write a story or a paragraph. Ideas are jotted down as they occur. Each idea is circled and linked to the main idea by a line. The student keeps adding ideas until he or she has put all of the important thoughts on the map. Then the instructor or study partner helps the writer put these ideas into the right sequence. This produces an outline to guide in writing the story or paragraph.

much more effective for LD learners than the traditional method of writing an outline down the page.

Keyboard Writing

In 1987 Joyce Steeves at Johns Hopkins University School of Education conducted extensive research with groups of adolescents who were dysgraphic and severely dyslexic. Steeves developed an index to show the rate of compensation for dysgraphia through keyboard writing. Her research determined that when severely dyslexic/dysgraphic learners are taught word processing skills, they can create 15 times more intelligent writing through a keyboard than by hand (cited by Jordan, 1989). The recent explosion of computer-based learning for those who are LD has given freedom of expression through keyboard writing that is impossible through penmanship. It is imperative that learners who are dysgraphic be taught keyboard writing strategies in place of traditional handwriting.

COMPENSATING FOR DYSCALCULIA

Chapter 8 reviewed the similarities between dyscalculia and other forms of dyslexia. Memory bridges are out along left brain pathways that transform number information into long-term memory. No matter how long or how hard these learners try, they do not develop long-term memory for the myriad facts and procedures of addition, subtraction, multiplication, and division. Learners with dyscalculia have no choice but to compensate.

Multisensory Processing

Learners with dyscalculia cannot do arithmetic or math silently. It is essential that they combine at least four sensory pathways at the same time. They must see/say/hear/touch in order to do even the simplest computation and problem solving. Chapter 8 demonstrated Brad and Andrea's multisensory processing (see Figure 8.7 and Figure 8.8). Both attended public school through 10th grade. Yet they cannot remember simple arithmetic processes. Their GED instructor developed a multisensory math program based upon touching and whispering to herself.

Tactile Math

The only way that learners with dyscalculia can do arithmetic computation is to involve the fingers in rhythmic movement. Tapping, touching, counting out loud, and tracing with the fingertips must be included. Several systems of "touch arithmetic" have been devised that teach the learner with dyscalculia to integrate seeing/touching/hearing/speaking as the framework for building mental images of number relationships and math processing. One of the most effective multisensory arithmetic systems is TIC TAC TOE developed by Richard Cooper who is himself dyslexic (Cooper, 1992). TIC TAC TOE shows the LD learner how number concepts fit together inside a grid. The learner with dyscalculia sees a picture of number relationships. Then the LD learner builds memory images of addition, subtraction, multiplication, and division by moving number patterns around inside the TIC TAC TOE grid. Cooper's tactile math method greatly enhances basic arithmetic for most learners with dyscalculia. TIC TAC TOE MATH is available through the Center for Alternative Learning, P.O. Box 716, Bryn Mawr, PA 19101.

Hand Calculator

Earlier in this chapter Steeve's research with severely dyslexic/dysgraphic adolescents who learned to compensate by writing through a word processor was presented. She discovered that these struggling learners could produce 15 times more and better writing with a keyboard than they could accomplish with pen or pencil. Educators are rapidly moving to word processing as the most efficient form of writing for all students. A similar compensation technique for learners who have dyscalculia is a hand calculator. This small keyboard device does for dyscalculia what a word processor does for dysgraphia. Punching keys enables those with math disability to compensate to a large degree for the crippling limits set by dyscalculia. Persons with deep dyslexia will continue to reverse number sequences as they use a hand calculator. But it is much easier for these LD learners to deal with math successfully when handwriting is not involved. Chapter 1 listed Kirsch's forecast of job requirements of the 21st century. All workers must deal with many types of keyboards even in the simplest kinds of work. Teaching students with dyscalculia to compensate with hand calculators is no longer an option.

CHAPTER 10

Attention Deficit Disorders

The concept of attention deficit among learners was slow coming into focus in our culture. In the 1920s and 1930s Orton, Slingerland, and other pioneers in the study of specific language disability (SLD) commented on nonverbal behaviors that included irritability, poor organization, quick frustration, short attention, unpredictable memory for details, trouble paying attention, and erratic learning of new information (Orton, 1925, 1937). In 1963 Samuel Clements presented the concept of MBD—*minimal brain dysfunction.* Clements postulated that because of minimal deficits in brain formation, certain learners could not maintain full attention or absorb new information consistently. They were always out of step with classmates and adult expectations. These MBD learners were overly irritable, too quickly frustrated, too impulsive, and too immature to fit into mainstream classrooms successfully (Clements, 1966). During the 1960s, Samuel Kirk's model of LD (learning disabilities) blended with Clements's concept of MBD to lay the foundation for the separate learning environments called Resource Rooms and Learning Labs that were established for youngsters who had these types of special learning needs.

DEFINITIONS OF ATTENTION DEFICIT

As special education programs for LD and MBD learners emerged during the 1970s, professional guidelines for diagnosing these patterns were developed by the American Psychiatric Association (APA). The *Diagnostic and Stastical Manual* (*DSM*) of the American Psychiatric Association became the standard by which professionals determined the existance of handicapping conditions related to poor school performance. In 1975 the term *attention deficit disorder* first appeared in APA *DSM II*. For the first time the professional world had clearly defined definitions of chronic inability to pay attention. APA *DSM II* established three categories of attentional deficit: (1) attention deficit disorder with hyperactivity; (2) attention deficit disorder without hyperactivity; and (3) attention deficit, residual type. By 1980 mental health professionals recognized that many children who were diagnosed as ADD gradually outgrew most of the symptoms as they matured during adolescence and early adulthood. Some did not. Certain individuals would become adults with all of the active patterns of attention deficit disorder they had displayed during childhood.

Those first attempts by the American Psychiatric Association to define attention deficits have gone through a series of changes as further research and professional experience have broadened our knowledge of attention deficits. In 1980 *DSM III* revised the definition of attention deficit to one main category: ADHD (attention deficit, hyperactive disorder). This sudden change in diagnosis triggered turmoil among diagnosticians who continued to see attention deficit without hyperactivity. In 1987 *DSM III-R* appeared with a further revision in the definition of attention deficit. The 1987 revision once more acknowleged that some individuals with attentional deficits are not hyperactive. In 1994 *DSM IV* presented still a different definition and classification of this behavior. *DSM IV* provided two domains (inattention and hyperactivity-impulsivity). Nevertheless, only one official label, attention-deficit/hyperactivity disorder, was designated. This bewildering fluctuation in the definitions and labeling of attention deficits reflects the broad differences of opinion within the professional community. In the 21st century, there will continue to be revisions in the guidelines for diagnosing attention deficits.

CAUSES OF ATTENTION DEFICIT DISORDER

In earlier chapters the science of brain imaging that allows one to watch the living brain at work was described. Two forms of brain imaging (PET [positron-emission tomography] and MRI [magnetic resonance imaging]) have disclosed differences in brain structure that lead to attention deficit disorders. During the 1980s Frank Wood discovered through PET scan studies that left brain blood flow is slower than normal in persons who are LD (Wood, 1991). In 1990 a research team led by Alan Zametkin reported that certain regions of the left cerebral cortex do not metabolize glucose adequately (see Figure 10.1). Zametkin and his colleagues discovered that this irregular glucose metabolism, along with irregular blood flow, triggers much of the hyperactivity and distractibility associated with ADHD [attention-deficit/hyperactive disorder] (Zemetkin, Nordahl, Gross, King, Semple, Rumsey, Hamburger, & Cohen, 1990). In 1991 Martha Denckla reported that her MRI research had identified immature structures within the cerebellum (Denckla, 1991). These differences in midbrain structure create the behaviors associated with ADD (attention deficit disorder without hyperactivity). These and other studies have determined that attention deficits originate in brain structures that are underdeveloped or that function irregularly.

ATTENTION DEFICIT IN ADULT EDUCATION

In spite of these fluctuations in how diagnosticans label attention deficit patterns, literacy providers face a practical issue: how to recognize attention deficits in adult learners and how to deal with this issue effectively. Chapter 1 presented the research that found 50 million undereducated adults in the American labor pool whose literacy skills are below 6th-grade level. Of this number, some 40 million are below 3rd-grade level in literacy skills. Of this group, some 30 million adults are LD. Within this vast population of adults with various forms of specific

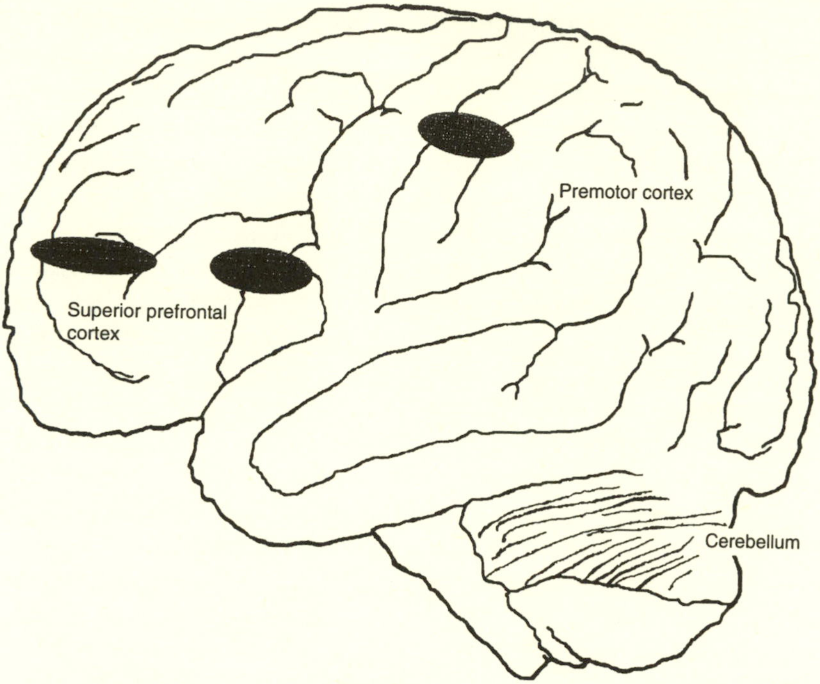

Figure 10.1. Areas of the left brain where glucose metabolism (sugar usage) is below normal in persons who have ADHD. Blood flow is also slower than normal. These regions of the left cerebral cortex do not receive enough fuel on a regular basis to do steady, consistent thought processing. Meanwhile, immature development of the cerebellum and limbic system of the midbrain causes poorly organized and very loose mental activity (Based upon models reported by Alan Zametkin et al., 1990; Frank Wood, 1991; and Martha Denckla, 1991.)

learning disability, many have attention deficit patterns that interfere with learning, job performance, and personal relationships (Jordan, 1992a, 1992b). These adults did not outgrow childhood and adolescent patterns of attention deficits. Today they enter adult education programs with the same kinds of attentional problems they have displayed all their lives.

ADHD—Attention Deficit, Hyperactive Disorder

Until 1994, attention deficit with hyperactivity (ADHD) was regarded mostly as a problem in learning new information. Even when teachers were irritated by impulsivity and short attention span, they could say: "Oh, well. Johnny is hyperactive." Somehow the term hyperactive allowed everyone to tolerate Johnny's behavior more easily. As the 1994 guidelines for diagnosing attention deficit appeared (APA *DSM IV*), a new point of view emerged. Based upon the extensive research of Russell Barkley, ADHD is now regarded as a disruptive behavior syndrome (Barkley, 1990). We are now aware that 65% of those diagnosed as ADHD also display overlapping patterns of oppositional defiant disorder (ODD). In addition, 30% of those diagnosed as ADHD also display symptoms of conduct disorder (CD). This new point of view brings hyperactive attention deficit behaviors into an increasingly negative light. It is much more difficult for instructors to tolerate behavior that is labeled disruptive.

ADHD Behaviors

The following behaviors are seen with attention-deficit, hyperactive disorder (ADHD):

Hyperactivity

- Excessive body activity. Squirms. Fidgets. Always on the go.
- Cannot leave others alone. Interrupts. Butts in. Intrudes.
- Cannot leave things alone. Always touching and handling.
- Cannot stay quiet. Talks excessively. Always commenting or blurting out.
- Constant body motion: rocking, bouncing, jiggling, shaking.
- Constantly making noise: rattling, clanking, clicking, slurping, rustling, bumping, drumming, humming.
- Rarely finishes what is started. Leaves a trail of unfinished tasks and projects.

Short Attention

- Cannot keep thoughts focused. Darts off on mental side trails.
- Must constantly be called back to the task.
- Does not finish. Quits to do something else.
- Too quickly bored. Wants something else to do. Too restless.

Loose Thought Patterns

- Cannot keep thoughts or mental images organized.
- Cannot keep on doing correct work. Begins to make careless mistakes after doing the first ones correctly.
- Cannot tell things in sequence. Thoughts jump around while telling. Events and facts are told out of sequence.
- Cannot follow instructions without jumping off track and skipping steps.

Impatience

- Has very little patience. Continually impatient. Cannot wait.
- No tolerance for standing in line or sitting still.
- Immediately irritable when forced to wait.
- Starts to fret and complain when required to wait.

Poor Organization

- Cannot keep own life organized.
- Loses things. Cannot remember where things were put.
- Forgets appointments. Usually late or does not show up.
- Personal space is cluttered and messy. Loses things inside the clutter.

Changes of First Impressions

- Mental images shift and change.
- Thinks others are playing tricks when own impressions change.
- Has it in mind, then loses it.
- Often surprised or startled as things seem different.

Poor Listening

- Continually misunderstands what is heard.
- Clamors to hear it again: "Huh? What? What do you mean?"
- Interrupts: "Huh? What do you mean?"

- Stops listening and starts paying attention to something else.
- Later blames others for not telling or saying it right.

Oversensitivity
- Overly defensive when criticized or corrected.
- Blames others instead of seeing own behavior.
- Spends much emotional energy arguing and defending self.
- Overreacts. Tantrums are out of proportion to what occurred.
- Jumps the gun. Does not wait to hear all the information before exploding or blaming.

Constant Distraction
- Stops work to see what others are doing.
- Cannot ignore own body sensations. Stops work to scratch, pick, rub, hitch clothing, examine something, rebutton, retie.
- Thoughts and attention dart everywhere instead of staying focused on task.

Immaturity
- Behaves like much younger person.
- Cannot get along with own age group.
- Interests, wishes, and thought patterns are like those of much younger persons.
- Makes no effort to grow up or become responsible.
- Lives mostly in a fantasy world. Ignores reality. Denies reality.
- Behavior is mostly impulsive. No evidence of common sense.
- Behavior is often compulsive. Things must be done in certain ways. Often develops rituals that must be followed.
- Acts on spur of the moment. Does not think things through.
- No regard for consequences.
- Self-focused. Puts self ahead of others. Wants own way now.
- Blames others instead of accepting responsibility.
- Triggers dislike and resentment in others.

Insatiable Behavior
- Desires are never satisfied. Clamors for more.
- Demands attention. Cannot leave others alone.
- No sense of privacy. Barges in on the privacy of others.

- Constantly bored. Demands something new or different.
- Complains that others get bigger share or more attention.
- Blames parents, spouse, colleagues, boss: "It's not fair!"
- Drains emotions of others by insatiable demands.
- Often dreaded and rejected by others.

Impulsive Behavior

- Does not plan ahead. Acts on spur of the moment.
- Shows no regard for consequences.
- Drawn to high risk behavior. Gets thrills from near accidents, bungee jumping, diving off cliffs, drag racing in the dark, high-speed driving in traffic, reckless driving.
- Places others in danger by breaking safety laws.

Disruptive Behavior

- Interrupts group situations.
- Keep things stirred up when others want to be quiet.
- Triggers conflicts in groups. Keeps arguments going over trivial issues.
- Disturbs neighbors in class, at home, in the community.
- No regard for social politeness. Clamors to get own way.
- Constantly makes noise. Feet scrub floor. Legs bump desk. Fingers tap or drum. Body squirms. Mouth makes noises.
- Inappropriate emotional responses. Laughs too loudly. Giggles too much. Has tantrums too often. Argues too much. Protests too frequently.

Oppositional Defiant Disorder (ODD)

According to research by Barkley and others, 65% of those who are diagnosed as being ADHD also display the following kinds of oppositional or defiant behaviors (Barkley, 1990).

- Habitually loses temper. Tantrums become a weapon to get one's own way.
- Automatically argues with authority.
- Actively defies or refuses to obey rules and regulations.
- Deliberately does things to annoy others.

- Automatically blames others regardless of what occurs.
- Is too touchy, too easily annoyed to get along with others.
- Is overly angry and resentful. Lives with a chip on the shoulder.
- Is openly spiteful and vindictive. Carries grudges. Refuses to forgive. Plots to get even.
- Automatically uses obscene or offensive language.

Conduct Disorder (CD)

From 20% to 30% of those who are diagnosed as being ADHD manifest symptoms of conduct disorder.

- Has history of secret stealing on more than one occasion (shoplifting, forgery, taking things without being seen).
- Has run away from home overnight at least twice while living with parents or surrogate parents.
- Automatically tells lies for no apparent reason.
- Has deliberately set fires.
- Has history of truancy from school or absence from work.
- Has history of breaking and entering homes, buildings, cars.
- Has deliberately destroyed property of others (other than setting fires).
- Has history of physical cruelty to animals.
- Has forced others into sexual activity.
- Has history of using weapons in fights.
- Has history of initiating fights.
- Has openly stolen from victims (mugging, purse snatching, extortion, armed robbery).
- Has history of being cruel to people.

ADD—Attention Deficit Disorder without Hyperactivity

Regardless of the labels used by diagnosticians, attention deficit without hyperactivity is prevalent in the adult population (Copeland, 1991; Hallowell & Ratey, 1994; Jordan,

1992b; Weiss & Hechtman, 1994). Adults with residual attention deficit often are passive, not hyperactive. Yet they have the same kind of difficulty maintaining attention long enough to finish what they start. Although hyperactive persons disrupt the learning environment, instructors do not have to guess when ADHD learners have darted off on mental rabbit trails. The body behavior (head turning, body turning, eyes turning) show where the lost attention has gone. Learners with ADD give almost no physical signals when their attention leaves the task. ADD is a passive, quiet occurrence that rarely attracts attention to itself. Students who are ADD can quietly drift along a different stream most of their educational years without teachers being aware. Those who are ADHD or ADD do plug into their environment now and then. During these plugged-in moments, they absorb most of what is happening. Then their plugs fall out and they are disengaged once more. Persons who are ADHD or ADD often make passing scores on tests because they have learned enough bits and pieces to guess successfully on multiple choice questions. Comprehensive exams that require extensive knowledge reveal the lack of information that normally accumulates over time.

ADD Behaviors

Passive Behavior

- Below normal body activity. Often appears lethargic.
- Reluctant to take part in group activities.
- Does not participate in group discussion.
- Avoids answering or giving oral responses.
- Rarely volunteers information or opinions.
- Prefers to stay alone during breaks.
- Avoids playing group games.
- Spends long periods of time alone in own private world.
- Uses fewest words possible when required to speak.
- Often appears "spacey" or disoriented.

Short Attention

- Quietly drifts away from task before finishing.
- Silently stops listening. Drifts away into own private world.

- Most of the time is off on private mental rabbit trails.
- Must continually be called back to finish tasks or to keep on listening.
- Appears surprised when attention comes back to task, like waking from a nap.
- Often says "Hmmm?" or "What?" when asked a question.

Loose Thought Patterns

- Cannot maintain organized mental images.
- Seems bewildered or confused as mental images fall apart.
- Begins making careless mistakes after doing the first items correctly.
- Cannot remember a series of facts or details.
- Loses words and stumbles over thoughts while telling.
- Cannot remember several steps in following instructions.
- Cannot remember assignments or projects over time unless reminded.
- Cannot remember game rules.
- Keeps forgetting names of people, places, things.

Poor Organization

- Continually loses or misplaces things.
- Cannot keep personal life organized without help.
- Cannot stay on schedule without supervision or reminding.
- Does not remember simple daily routines.
- Lives or works in cluttered, messy personal space.
- Cannot clean up or reorganize clutter without help.

Change of First Impressions

- First impressions do not stay the same. Mental images shift to something different.
- Stops whatever is being done when mental images shift. Appears puzzled, bewildered, confused as impressions change.
- Cannot keep doing a series of things the same way. Spelling deteriorates. Math accuracy deteriorates. Loses the sequence of steps while doing tasks.
- Expresses surprise when attention comes back into focus.

Poor Listening Comprehension

- Does not absorb full meaning of what others say. Often says "Hmmm?" or "What?" or "I don't understand."

- Must hear oral instructions again.
- Does not keep on listening. Begins to drift away into own world instead of continuing to listen.
- Eyes develop a far-away look as attention drifts away.
- Spends much time daydreaming or "star gazing" instead of participating.
- Listens too poorly to keep up with current events or local news
- Does not get the point of jokes.

Time Lag in Processing
- Long pauses before reacting.
- Must be reminded or guided to start doing assignments.
- Long periods of time with nothing done. Sits silently doing nothing.
- Long periods of time spent searching memory. Very slow retrieving learned information.
- Continual soft whispering to self while searching memory or doing tasks.
- Cannot keep up with the group. Always behind class schedule.

Unfinished Tasks
- Rarely finishes what is started.
- Believes tasks are finished whenever attention drifts away.
- Does not realize when more is yet to be done to finish tasks.

Poor Socialization Skills
- Too shy and insecure to develop small talk or chit-chat skills.
- Does not listen well enough to be good at conversation.
- Does not keep up with local news or current events well enough to join discussions.

Easily Distracted
- Quietly pays more attention to what goes on nearby than to own tasks.
- Stops work to wonder what others are doing.
- Thoughts continually drift to personal issues not related to the task at hand: family finances; health problems; welfare of

children; television programs; emotions left over from events at home.

Lack of Continuity

- Personal life does not have a sense of continuity.
- Lives from moment to moment, one event to the next.
- Does not perceive how one event flows into the next event.
- Must have supervision to stay with a plan or program.

Poor Telling and Describing

- Speech is slow and halting as person searches for next words.
- Bogs down while telling. Stumbles over names, places, facts.
- Speech is made up of fragments instead of whole statements.
- Others become impatient waiting for person to say it.

VISIBLE SIGNS OF ATTENTION DEFICIT

These checklists present many invisible behavioral signs that indicate when a person has attention deficit disorder. Other visible signs of ADHD or ADD also can be observed in the paper trail students leave behind in school files and on daily assignments.

Doodling

Figure 10.2 is an example of elaborate doodling that we often see when a learner is ADHD or ADD. Doodling is a compensation strategy that channels excess internal energy or nervousness onto paper. When ADHD learners doodle, their fingers drain away a type of internal static. While doodling, these individuals can listen much better without losing attentional focus.

Bar Graph Scatter

Figure 10.3 shows the unique attention deficit scatter of bar graphs from standardized achievement tests. Each bar on

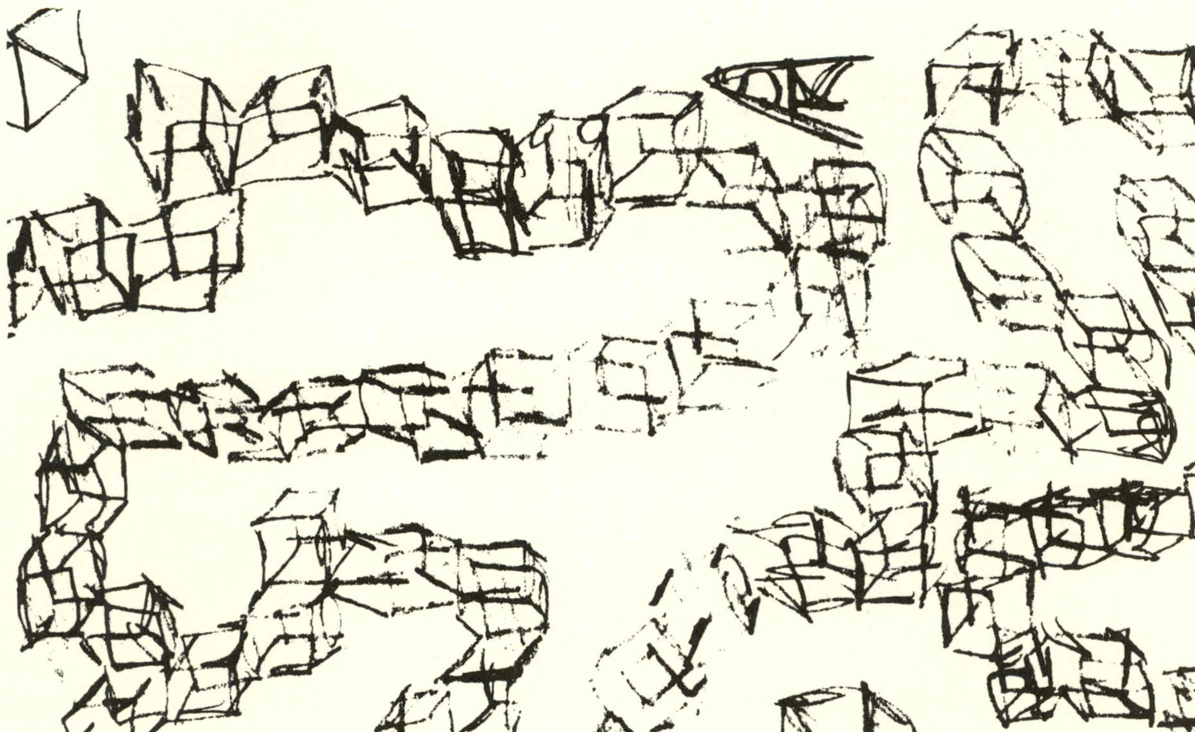

Figure 10.2. John has developed this elaborate doodling system that transfers enough random mental energy through his fingers onto paper to enable him to listen well for long periods of time. If he stops doodling, his ability to listen falls apart.

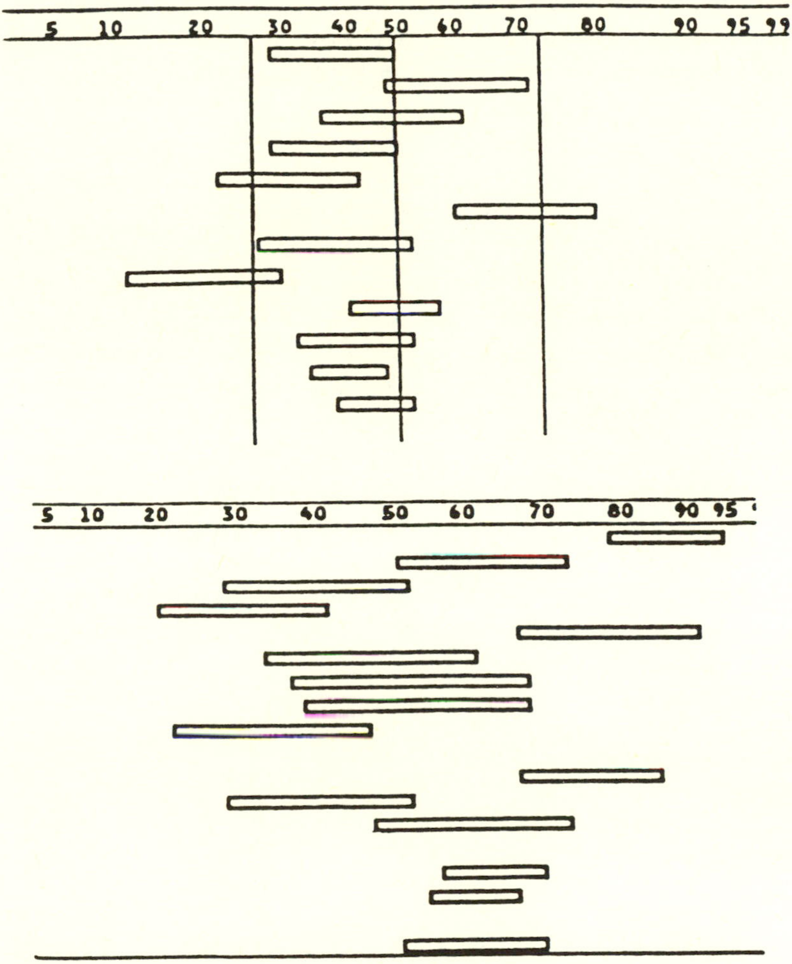

Figure 10.3. Attention deficit is indicated by the wide scatter of bars on this kind of graph from standardized achievement tests. The numbers across the top of the graphs represent percentile levels. Fluctuation in attention span while taking each subtest causes wide differences in levels of performance throughout the test battery. ADD/ADHD inattention is reflected by the constant change of percentile ranking. Some subtests range from 30th percentile to 50th percentile. Other subtests range from 10th percentile 30th percentile. When attention is under full control, percentile range is as high as 80th to 95th level.

the graph represents a timed segment of the test. The wide scatter throughout the graph indicates how much loss of attention occurred while the student struggled through the timed test battery.

Subscore Scatter

Part of the clinical diagnosis of ADHD or ADD is a standardized intelligence test, usually the Wechsler Intelligence Scale. This intelligence test consists of 11 subtests. Each subtest attempts to measure a different kind of mental ability. Figure 10.4 shows the kind of wide scatter among the Wechsler subtests when the person is ADHD or ADD. Unfortunately, very bright ADHD or ADD individuals are not always given credit for the high scores inside the Wechsler subscore scatter. When the bottom scores are averaged with the high scores, a highly intelligent ADD or ADHD person can be labeled "average" in mental ability. Those who interpret standardized tests must always look for the inside scatter of the subscores. Figure 10.4 shows a typical score scatter that indicates attention deficit, not average intelligence.

Unfinished Work

As we have seen in the ADHD and ADD checklists, unfinished work is a major sign of attention deficit. Whether the student is ADHD or ADD, he or she stops working whenever the attention moves away. At that point the student believes that all the work is finished. Figure 10.5 illustrates this sign of attention deficit on math assignments. After working the first few problems correctly, both students "lost it" and could not remember how to do the next few problems. While doing these math assignments, each student drifted away and had to be reminded repeatedly to finish. When the instructor reminded, these students were surprised. "I thought I was through," they said each time.

The Impact of Make Believe

Instructors often wonder where attention goes when it leaves the task. To understand the impact of ADHD and ADD on the learning process, we must understand the role of make believe. When the learner's attention darts away (ADHD) or drifts away (ADD), that person is no longer part of the reality of that situation. Without warning the ADHD or ADD individual has entered his or her private world of fantasy and make believe. Persons with ADHD may not stay longer than a few seconds inside their world of make believe. Those who are ADD often spend many minutes at a time off in that invisible world they share with no one else. But during those absent moments, these distractible individuals are in another world: "I wonder. . . . What if. . . . .I wish. . . . .Do you suppose. . . . ." This is the world of make believe that draws ADHD and ADD learners away from the task. If instructors listen carefully without interrupting, they can peek through verbal windows to get quick glimpses of these invisible worlds of fantasy. A hyperactive man will talk excitedly about the 4-wheel drive truck he dreams of owning. He describes it vividly and knows every detail of his dream truck. Meanwhile, he may have lost his job or failed the GED because he spends so much time dreaming about his fantasy vehicle. A passive woman may quietly talk about a dreamy romance based upon a character in a favorite soap opera or television program. If she feels confident with her listener, she may shyly describe the details of this imagined romance. For a moment the listener sees inside the private place where this ADD student spends much of her time instead of finishing assignments or carrying out responsibilities. The invisible realm of make believe is often the most dynamic part of life for adults who are ADHD or ADD.

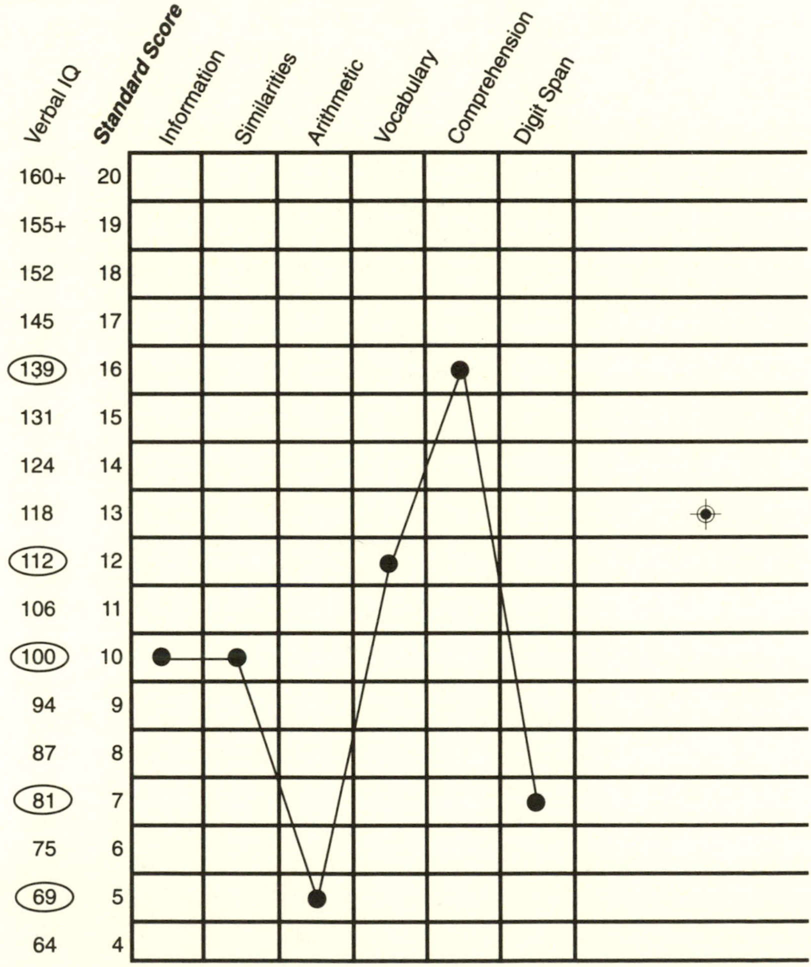

Verbal IQ
Standard Score
Information
Similarities
Arithmetic
Vocabulary
Comprehension
Digit Span
160+ 20
155+ 19
152 18
145 17
139 16
131 15
124 14
118 13
112 12
106 11
100 10
94 9
87 8
81 7
75 6
69 5
64 4

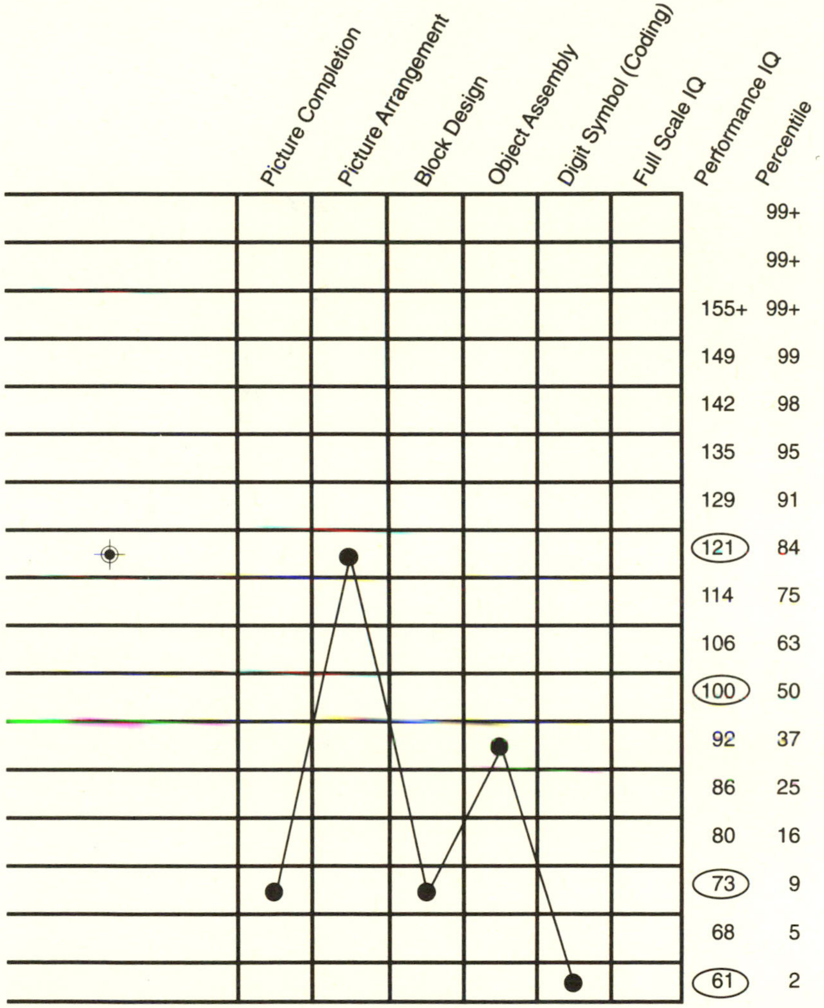

Figure 10.4. Attention deficit is indicated by the very wide scatter of subtest scores on the Wechsler Intelligence Test.

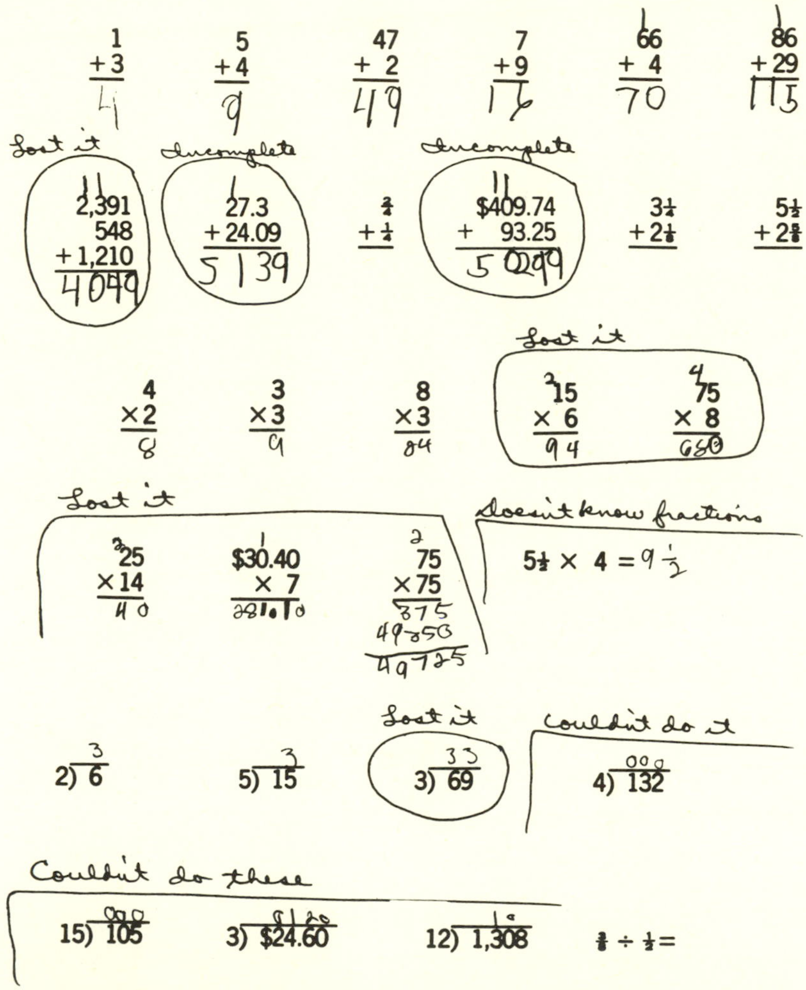

Figure 10.5. Attention deficit is seen in this erratic, incomplete work by two adults with ADD. Each has a good foundation in arithmetic computation, but loose thought patterns and drifting away from the task interfere with their performance. Attention deficit often appears to be lack of knowledge. However, these students do know arithmetic facts when their attention is fully focused and they can stay on task.

CHAPTER 11

How to Compensate for Attention Deficits

Chapter 10 presented the underlying causes for attention deficit disorders: irregular glucose metabolism and slow blood flow in the left brain, as well as immature development within the cerebellum. Specific behavior patterns seen when a person is hyperactive (ADHD) or when there is no hyperactivity (ADD) were described. These residual behaviors have existed since birth for the ADHD and ADD adults who desire further education. It has never been easy for these struggling learners to succeed in the classroom. In spite of being quite intelligent, they rarely have been regarded as good students. They think of themselves as being "dumb" in comparison with classmates who always make better grades. They rarely have enough patience to stay with tasks long enough to build better literacy skills. They are often unrealistic in what they expect from adult education. They disrupt traditional classes by being hyperactive or spending too much time drifting silently away. In earlier chapters the unmistakable signs of dyslexia and poor visual perception were listed. Instructors have little trouble recognizing those visible barriers to learning. But attention deficit patterns are mostly invisible, making it harder for instructors to recognize and understand. Nevertheless, it is possible to develop compensation strategies that can enable adults with ADHD and ADD to reach educational goals.

PINPOINT SPECIFIC STUMBLING BLOCKS

It is essential that instructors know what they are facing as they work with adults who have attention deficits. The first step must be to develop a checklist of behaviors the instructor encounters in teaching these learners. By completing this kind of checklist survey, teachers and tutors will be better prepared to do the continual reminding, coaching, and forgiving that are required if ADHD and ADD learners are to succeed. An especially helpful tool in identifying specific attentional patterns is the *Jordan Executive Function Index* (Jordan, 1992a). This instrument surveys how well or how poorly the student pays attention, organizes his or her life, and controls impulses. This information allows the instructor and the student to pinpoint specific strengths and weaknesses that must be recognized if the learner is to be successful.

REMINDER SYSTEMS

It is imperative that learners who are ADHD and ADD develop some type of reminder system to keep them on track. One of the most urgent needs these strugglers face is to remember what to do and when to do it. The nature of attention deficit makes it impossible for these individuals to hold complete mental images over a period of time. They must have some kind of outside system to remind them often enough to keep them on schedule at work, in the classroom, and in their daily lives.

Assignment Notebook

ADHD and ADD learners must develop the habit of carrying a small notebook in which they jot down every assignment, appointment, and obligation. A pocket size notebook that easily slips into a purse or a pocket will do. This notebook becomes the supervisor. The adult with ADHD or ADD is coached over and over in how to depend on this notebook that reminds the person of every important event. All class assignments are written. All appointments are noted hour by hour and day by day. Persons with attention deficits who succeed live by this kind of pocket log that reminds them without scolding or nagging. Especially forgetful individuals have trouble keeping track of their notebooks. Some extremely forgetful persons keep backup copies of their schedules to have when the originals are misplaced. One of the first goals in teaching adults with ADHD or ADD is to develop a reminder system that includes a pocket notebook.

Personal Timer

Few persons who are ADHD or ADD have an automatic awareness of time. They do not have an inward sense of how much time is passing. They are dependent on outside time reminders. A major goal of teaching adults with this type of LD is to guide them in developing a personal timer system. Every person who is ADHD or ADD should invest in a computer wristwatch that can be programmed to beep at selected times. In the 21st century, having one's own personal timer will be as affordable as a pair of shoes. Adults who are ADHD or ADD should regard this compensatory strategy as essential to their success. Wearing a beeper on the arm or in a pocket should become a natural part of their lives.

COMPENSATING FOR ADHD AND ADD IN THE CLASSROOM

Possibly the most pressing goal of each instructor is to reduce disruptive ADHD and ADD patterns as much as possible. Adult education centers can develop ways for excess body energy to be absorbed so that other learners are not disturbed.

Doodling

In Chapter 10 there is an example of doodling by an ADHD adult (see Figure 10.2). Many students who are ADHD live with inner tension that keeps them nervous and on edge most of the time. This inner tension interrupts their ability to listen. These persons often benefit from doodling. As the fingers grip the pencil, much of the inner distraction flows into the doodle pattern as it emerges on the page. Most persons who doodle listen more effectively than when their fingers are idle. Doodling is also effective in controlling the urge to touch or handle or fiddle with things. Students with restless fingers that want to reach for whatever is nearby can control this impulse through doodling. When doodling is encouraged as part of a classroom compensation strategy, a good deal of irritation and conflict can be removed from the environment. Doodling provides a sanctioned form of release and redirection of inner tension that soon gets the ADHD learner into trouble in the classroom.

Squeeze Objects

Every adult education classroom should have a variety of squeeze objects. Wise instructors lay soft rubber balls and other squeeze toys on work tables and in library corners. The need to keep fingers busy is satisfied in a remarkably soothing, comfortable way when ADHD learners are free to squeeze and manipulate things without disturbing neighbors. Squeeze objects silently absorb incredible amounts of ADHD tension. This strategy helps to maintain a quieter, less active learning environment for everyone.

Chewing

Most learners who are ADHD have overpowering urges to chew as they concentrate. Adult classrooms should encourage quiet chewing as a release for inner tension. Rules should be clearly established about where to put gum wrappers and where to discard used gum. Rules should also regulate disruptive behaviors like slurping, blowing bubbles, or making chewing sounds. Rhythmic chewing offers the same kind of release that doodling and squeezing provide. Encouraging quiet chewing promotes a quieter learning environment with less buildup of disruptive inner tension.

Moveable Chairs

When possible, adult learning centers should have student chairs on casters. Enormous tension develops in the large muscles of ADHD adults who are required to sit in typical classroom chairs. Within a few minutes the thighs and buttocks become so stressed the person must move about. When ADHD is confined to immovable furniture, body squirming is inevitable. Within a short time pent-up stress must be released. In traditional classrooms with fixed or immovable furniture, this confinement generates conflict as hyperactive squirming, heaving, and thrashing about occurs. Sturdy chairs on casters permit release of body tension without creating too much conflict.

Carpeted Spaces

Classrooms and study areas for adults who are ADHD should have carpeted spaces to absorb the sounds of foot scrubbing and toe thumping that are inevitable. ADHD learners should always work on these carpeted spaces. Chairs on casters are virtually silent when they are placed on carpet. A few oversize pillows, large beanbags, and sofa cushions should be available around the room. Restless students should be encouraged to lie on the floor, stand at the table, or take whatever position keeps them relaxed. The classroom rule is that those who move do so quietly. Being free to move or change body position every few minutes is critical in draining away excess energy.

Task Timers

Many adult learners carry deep dread of doing tasks that are timed. A form of school phobia can escalate into a panic attack when certain students realize that they are being timed. Other learners have no sense of time and therefore cannot regulate their use of time. Adult classrooms should provide silent timers for those who need visual reminders of time passing. It is possible to find silent timers that do not tick or whir. Many instructors use sand timers that empty every three or five minutes. Students who are ADHD and ADD must face the issue of time. Their lives will confront them with situations that are closely timed. The adult education classroom should coach these learners to stretch their attention span by using timers. If the student can maintain full attention for two minutes before losing mental images, the goal should be to work with a three-minute timer to stretch attention span to that limit. Gradually most short-attention persons can build longer tolerance for concentration. Those who fear working under timed conditions should practice reading, writing, or doing math assignments with a quiet or silent timer. This is a form of desensitizing old fears.

Written Outlines

One of the challenges of ADHD and ADD is keeping up with new information. Too many gaps occur during the moments when attention is distracted or the person drifts away. The most efficient strategy to bridge these gaps is for the instructor to provide simple outlines of all new information. Once each ADHD or ADD student has the outline, he or she can be reminded to go back to that list whenever thought patterns jump track. Oral instructions should never be given without also giving a written outline or summary. Lectures should follow the outline that has been given to each learner. These class outlines will supplement the assignment notebook system of reminding.

Tape Recorders

Some students prefer to have a recording of what was said in addition to following written outlines. It takes only a few moments for an instructor to speak the instructions and other information into a tape recorder. Then ADHD and ADD learners can hear the information as many times as they need. This provides a double system for reviewing new information. Each adult classroom should permit or provide the use of tape recorders to give a multisensory system for reviewing new information.

Study Partners

Few students who are ADHD or ADD can study effectively by themselves. Alone, they flounder because too many gaps emerge in their knowledge. By themselves, they have no outside source to remind and coach them. These learners need the immediate feedback that comes from a study partner. Most students who are LD make much better progress by doing at least part of their learning with a partner who listens, then gives immediate feedback.

Extended Time

In the discussions of dyslexia and dysgraphia the need for enough time was emphasized. Many students who are ADHD or ADD also need extra time to do their best. It is essential for hyperactive persons to take many short breaks. If they try to repress inner tension in order to stay on task, their emotions reach a point of exploding. These episodes are called overload or burnout. Instructors can avoid these disruptive explosions by making sure that struggling learners have plenty of time. Extending time by 15 to 20 minutes to let the student take frequent breaks often is enough to avoid burnout or emotional overload.

Personal Reminding

Earlier the factor of daydreaming or stargazing in students who are ADD was covered. Without warning their thoughts drift silently away from the task. These silent drifters may be absent from their task for long periods of time unless an outsider kindly brings them back. Instructors must be willing to remind ADD learners by quietly calling their names or touching them gently on the shoulder. When the student's attention has returned, the instructor takes a moment to help the learner find the place again. This reminding is never done in a critical spirit. Every effort is made to avoid embarrassing the learner who is ADD. Without this kind of personal reminding, it is often impossible for the individual with attention deficits to succeed in the classroom.

Eye Contact

The following is a rule of thumb for teaching those with ADHD and ADD: Never expect them to listen until they have established eye contact with the speaker. Sometimes it is necessary to touch the person's shoulder in order to bring eye contact to the speaker's face. If a major moment of distraction has occurred in which the attention has been strongly pulled away, the instructor must wait for the distraction cycle to finish before the learner is ready to listen.

Waiting without Interrupting

Persons who are ADHD often display a pattern that is difficult to understand. They usually describe this as "playing a tape in my head." The individual begins to tell or describe an event. The words go on and on. It is time for the person to end the story. But the ADHD person cannot stop talking before "finishing the tape." If these individuals are interrupted while their inner voice tape is playing, they are intensely frustrated, even angry. Many of the outbursts that instructors witness are triggered when others interrupt before the ADHD tape has finished playing. As much as possible, instructors must let these invisible inner voice tapes finish playing before interrupting. To interrupt is to startle the person so much that he or she becomes angry or hostile.

MEDICATION FOR ADHD AND ADD

Instructors in adult education should be aware of medications that are frequently prescribed for learners with residual ADHD and ADD. When APA *DSM II* introduced the term attention deficit disorder in 1975, only a few medications were available to improve the thought patterns of attention deficit disorder. Then the most frequently used cortical stimulants were Ritalin (methylphenidate), Cylert (Pemoline), and Dexedrine (Dextroamphetamine). When used in correct dosage levels, those medications usually lengthened attention span, reduced distractibility, improved memory for details, and increased listening ability. Today a broad range of medications are available to reduce the frustrations of ADHD and ADD. Persons who have carried attention deficits into adulthood respond just as well to cortical stimulants as do children and adolescents. When used wisely at lower dosage levels, adults with ADHD and ADD often find themselves learning more effectively than ever before in their school experience. Appendix A shows the medications most frequently used to treat attention deficit disorders.

CHAPTER 12

The Future for LD Adults in America

As the United States approaches the 21st century, the issue of learning disabilities in our culture is filled with irony. Since 1973 our society has developed a comprehensive body of legislation to safeguard the interests and needs of those who are LD. Peter and Patricia Latham have published two volumes that summarize current law designed to protect the interests of LD citizens: *Attention Deficit Disorder and the Law: A Guide for Advocates* (1992) and *Learning Disabilities and the Law* (1993). These volumes are guidelines for all who have an interest in the rights of children, adolescents, and adults who struggle to learn. As these impressive advocates make clear, our culture does not lack legal protection for those who learn differently. Within the legal profession a new specialty has emerged. Those who are LD are supported by a vigorous band of advocates who are determined that this body of legal protection will be enforced.

In the 1950s a grassroots movement began through parents of children whose learning differences were not adequately recognized by American public education. Out of that parent concern emerged ACLD—Association for Children with Learning Disabilities. Today this vital organization is called LDA—Learning Disabilities Association. At the same time another group of advocates, The Orton Dyslexia Society, has grown into an influential body of professionals with vital interests in specific learning disabilities. During the 1980s parents of children with attention deficit disorders organized CH.A.A.D., an active society supporting the rights and needs of those with ADHD and ADD. Many similar advocate groups now exist to press for legal, educational, and social support of Americans who are LD. The 21st century will offer a broad range of protective laws and policies at every level of government.

How, then, has the American culture produced 50 million subliterate adults? How have U.S. schools and communities poured 40 million illiterate citizens into the workplace? How have 30 million adults with untreated learning disabilities been permitted to enter the workplace unprepared for the job requirements of the future? These questions stagger our nation. No one saw this tidal wave of educational need approaching. Passing protective laws since 1973 did not prevent vast numbers of bright strugglers from falling through the cracks.

In spite of this sober reality, the future for LD learners in America can be bright and hopeful. The causes of learning disabilities, learning differences, learning difficulties, and late development of learning ability were presented in preceding chapters. Technology is already here to permit LD learners to compensate and thrive when accommodations are provided. On the horizon are new technologies that will permit individuals who are LD to bypass their differences almost completely. Working models of encoding devices that listen to human speech, edit for grammar and spelling, then print the text in finished form already exist. In the near future these electronic miracles will remove most of the barriers our educational customs have erected against those who are LD. Not far into the next century there will be easy access to communication technologies that will remove old stigmas and obstacles for those who are dyslexic. Within two or three more decades a predominently oral culture will have technologies that readily turn speech into writing. Those who cannot read will see what they need to know on incredible video screens. Those who cannot spell will dictate to electronic scribes. Those who cannot write will tell their thoughts to encoders that will process oral messages into print. New medications and tailored diets will smooth the roughness out of attention deficits so that those intelligent individuals can participate effectively in their societies. Interactive computer networks already link homes, classrooms, and work places worldwide. The potential for meeting the special needs of LD learners is very bright indeed.

America stands at a critical fork in the road. Do we as a nation and society turn in generosity in the direction of reaching out to those with special needs? Do we implement our vast body of knowledge and technology to reclaim the lost talent at the bottom of the labor pool and make sure that future learners succeed? Or do we turn toward a conservative direction that withholds this kind of support from others? Do we in effect decide that we are not actually our brother's keeper beyond a meager point of helping?

In a bewildering manner, American society is moving in two directions at the same time as we try to accommodate the special needs of learning differences. As the Lathams have eloquently written, society continues to move ahead in developing the law on behalf of citizens who have special needs. Americans with Disabilities Act (ADA) has come into the workplace determined that everyone be treated fairly. Educators at all levels are well aware of their responsibilities under such statutes as the Rehabilitation Act of 1973 and the Individuals with Disabilities Education Act that was born in 1975. Human resources directors in industry, managers of businesses large and small, and those who manage our schools have no doubt about our duties toward those with special needs.

But the workplace has yet to open its doors to those who are LD. As American industry has downsized to compete with other world markets, an alarming trend has become the rule. Virtually all employers today have literacy standards that shut out most of those who need accommodation. In chapter 1 I reviewed the workplace of the future where workers at all levels must process fast moving information from many sources: computer screens, keyboards, electronic communication systems, and databases. To become employed at a living wage, future workers must score high school reading levels to be considered for a job. It is not unusual for industries or business to require reading achievement scores at 12th-grade level for everyone in that workforce, from custodians to upper management. Fast food chains require rapid data processing and the ability to cope with volumes of oral information without mistake. Manual labor such as loading trucks or stocking warehouses increasingly requires knowledge of computer codes and streams of symbols. The workplace seems to move directly opposite the direction our legal structure says we ought to go.

At this time America has not decided what to do with the challenge of LD. Public education is torn between continuing to shelter struggling learners in supportive Resource Rooms, or following the call of full inclusion that would return different learners to the mainstream. The public cry to reduce federal government is not yet demanding that local funding replace federal aid. So we stand at a fork in the road, not quite sure how to put into motion all of the splendid potential for accommodating LD.

This study began with the observation that the 50 million subliterates in the workforce did not suddenly appear one day. They dropped one by one throught the cracks of the educational and social systems. To bring these intelligent ones back, we must reach out one by one to reclaim them. As individuals, we who know how must reach out to individuals who have not yet learned. That is the hope for our future.

APPENDIX A

Medications for ADHD and ADD

Drug	Possible Side Effects	Benefits	Precautions
Ritalin Methyl-phenidate	Insomnia, loss of appetite, weight loss, headache, irritability, stomachache	less distraction better listening longer attention better memory	Not for patients with marked anxiety, motor tics, history of Tourette syndrome
Dexedrine Dextro-amphetamine	Insomnia, loss of appetite, weight loss, headache, irritability, stomachache	Reduces hyperactivity. Lengthens attention span	Not for patients with marked anxiety, motor tics, history of Tourette syndrome
Cylert Pemoline	Insomnia, agitation headache, stomachache, abnormal liver function tests	Improved attention better concentration better long-term memory	Not for patients with history of liver problems
Tofranil Imipramine Hydrochloride	Dry mouth, loss of appetite, headache, stomachache, mild irregular heart beat, dizziness, constipation	Relieves anxiety and depression	Not for patients with history of heart problems

Norpramin Desipramine Hydrochloride	Dry mouth, loss of appetite, headache, stomachache, mild irregular heart beat, dizziness, constipation	Relieves anxiety and depression	Not for patients with history of heart problems
Catapres Clonidine Hydrochloride	Sleepiness, nausea, headache, dry mouth, stomachache, low blood pressure, dizziness	Relieves tic disorder, severe aggression, severe hyperactivity	
Prozac	Depression, thoughts of dying	Relieves anxiety, controls panic attacks	
Anafranil		Stops chronic fretting and excessive worry	

REFERENCES

American Psychiatric Association. (1975). *Diagnostic and statistical manual of mental disorders* (2nd ed.). Washington, DC: Author.

American Psychiatric Association. (1980). *Diagnostic and statistical manual of mental disorders* (3rd ed.). Washington, DC: Author.

American Psychiatric Association. (1987). *Diagnostic and statistical manual of mental disorders* (3rd ed. rev.). Washington, DC: Author.

American Psychiatric Association. (1994). *Diagnostic and statistical manual of mental disorders* (4th ed.). Washington, DC: Author.

Barkley, R. A. (1990). *Attention deficit hyperactive disorder: A handbook for diagnosis and treatment.* New York: Guilford.

Bastian, C. H. (1869). On the various forms of loss of speech in cerebral disease. *The British Medico-Chirurgical Review,* 43, 209–236, 470–494.

Beasley, G. F. (1995). *Center for excellence: Learning disabilities in the workplace,* pp. 2–3. Crossett, AR: Georgia-Pacific Corporation.

Berlin, R. (1884). Uber Dyslexie. *Archiv fur Psychiatrie,* 15, 276–278.

Blakeslee, S. (1994, August 16). New clue to cause of dyslexia seen in mishearing of fast sounds. *The New York Times,* pp. C1, C10.

Clements, S. D. (1966). *Minimal brain dysfunction in children*, Monograph No. 3, U.S. Department of H.E.W., Public Health Service Bulletin No. 1415, NINDS, Washington, DC.

Cooper, R. (1992). *TIC TAC TOE MATH*: An Alternative method for learning problem adults. Bryn Mawr, PA: Learning DisAbilities Consultants.

Copeland, E. D. (1991). *Medications for attention disorders (ADHD ADD) and related medical problems.* Atlanta, GA: SPI Press.

Denckla, M. B. (1991, February 25). *The neurology of social competence.* Paper presented at the Learning Disabilities Association National Conference, Chicago.

Drake, C. (1989). The terminology trap. In R. E. Cohen, & J. C.

Neeley (Eds.), *Learning disability law* (pp. 2–4). New York: Committee on Juvenile Justice, Dyslexia, and Other Language Disabilities of the Appellate Division of the Supreme Court of the State of New York.

Duane, D. D. (1985, November). Psychiatric implications of neurological difficulties. Symposium conducted at the Menninger Foundation, Topeka, KS.

Evans, M. M. (1982). *Dyslexia: An annotated bibliography.* Westport, CT: Greenwood.

Galaburda, A. M. (1983). Developmental dyslexia: Current anatomical research. *Proceedings of the 33rd annual conference of The Orton Dyslexia Society, Annals of Dyslexia,* 33, 41–54.

Galaburda, A. M. (1985). Developmental dyslexia: A review of biological interactions. *Annals of Dyslexia,* 35, 21–33.

Gall, F. J., & Spurzheim, J. C. (1809). *Untersuchungen über die Anotomie des Nervensystems überhaupt und des Gehirns insebesondere.* Paris, Strassburg: Treuttel & Wurtz.

Geiger, G., & Lettvin, J. Y. (1987). Peripheral vision in persons with dyslexia. *The New England Journal of Medicine,* 316 (20) 1238–1243.

Geschwind, N., & Levitsky, W. (1968). Human brain: Left-right asymmetries in temporal speech region. *Science,* 161, 186–187.

Geschwind, N. (1984). The biology of dyslexia: The after-dinner speech. In D. B. Gray & J. F. Kavanagh (Eds.), *Biobehavioral measures of dyslexia* (pp. 1–19). Parkton, MD: York.

Goldsheider, A. (1892). *Über centrale Sprach-Schreib-und Lesestörungen. Berliner Klinishe Wochenschrift,* 29, 64–66, 100–102, 122–125, 144–147, 168–171.

Grashey, H. (1885). Über Aphasie und ihre Beziehung zur Wahrnehmung. *Archiv für Psychiatrie,* 16, 654–688.

Hallowell, E. M., & Ratey, J. J. (1994). *Driven to distraction: Recognizing and coping with attention deficit disorder from childhood through adulthood.* New York; Pantheon.

Hammill, D. D. (1990). On defining learning disabilities: An emerging consensus. In *Journal of Learning Disabilities,* 23 (2) 74–83.

Harris, T. (1970). National reading council studies as cited in Jordan, 1989.

Hinshelwood, J. (1900). Congenital word-blindness. *The Lancet,* 1, 1506–1508.

Irlen, H. (1991). *Reading by the colors: Overcoming dyslexia and other reading disabilities through the Irlen method.* Garden City Park, NY: Avery.

Jordan, D. R. (1972). *Dyslexia in the classroom.* Columbus, OH: Merrill.

Jordan, D. R. (1988). *Jordan prescriptive/tutorial reading program for moderate and severe dyslexics.* Austin, TX: PRO-ED.

Jordan, D. R. (1989). *Overcoming dyslexia in children, adolescents, and adults.* Austin, TX: PRO-ED.

Jordan, D. R. (1992a). Jordan executive function index for adults. In D. R. Jordan *Attention deficit disorder: ADHD and ADD syndromes.* Austin, TX: PRO-ED.

Jordan, D. R. (1992b). *Attention deficit disorder: ADHD and ADD syndromes.* Austin, TX: PRO-ED.

Kidder, C. B. (1991). Dyslexia and adult illiteracy: Forging the missing link. *The Lantern,* (p. 1). Prides Crossing: Landmark School.

Kirsch, I. S., Jungeblut, A., & Campbell, A. (1992). *Beyond the school doors: The literacy needs of job seekers served by the U.S. department of labor.* Princeton: Educational Testing Service.

Kirsch, I. S. (1992a). *Adult literacy in america.* Princeton, NJ: Educational Testing Service.

Kirsch, I. S., Jungeblut, A., Jenkins, L., & Kolstad, A. (1992b). *Adult literacy in america: A first look at the results of the national adult literacy survey.* Princeton, NJ: Educational Testing Service.

Korhonen, L. J. (1975). Handbook for learning disabilities and the adult basic education student. *Staff Development Bulletin*, Region V, *3* (2), 19–36. Urbana, IL: School Management Institute, Inc.

Kozol, J. (1985). *Illiterate america.* New York: New American Library.

Latham, P. S., & Latham, P. H. (1992). *Attention deficit disorder and the law: A guide for advocates.* Washington, DC: JKL Communications.

Latham, P. S., & Latham, P. H. (1993). *Learning disabilities and the law.* Washington, DC: JKL Communications.

Laubach Literacy Action. (1994). *Teaching adults: A literacy resource book.* Syracuse: New Readers Press.

Lehmkuhle, S., Garzia, R. P., Turner, L., Hash, T., & Baro, J. A. (1993). A defective visual pathway in children with reading disability. *New England Journal of Medicine,* 328 (14) 989–996.

Lichtheim, L. (1885). On aphasie. *Brain,* 7, 432–484.

Leisman, G. (1976). *Basic visual processes and learning disability.* Springfield, IL: Thomas.

Livingstone, M. S., Rosen, G. D., Drislane, F. W., & Galaburda, A. M. (1991). Physiological and anatomical evidence for a magnocellular deficit in developmental dyslexia. *Proceedings of the National Academy of Science, USA,* 88 (9) 7943–7947.

Meynert, Th. (1868). Die Bedeutung des Gehirns fur das Vorstellungsleben. In Th. Meynert (Ed.), *Sammlung von populärwissenschaftlichen Vortägen xber den Bau und die Leistungen des Gehirns* (pp. 3–16).Wien and Lepizig, Austria: Braunmuller.

Montgomery, G. (1989). The mind in motion. *Discover,* 10 (3) 58–68.

National Commission on Excellence in Education. (1983). *A nation at risk: The imperative for educational reform.* Washington, DC: National Commission on Excellence in Education.

National Joint Committee on Learning Disabilities (1988) cited in D. D. Hammill (1990). On defining learning disabilities: An emerging consensus. In *Journal of Learning Disabilities.* 23 (2) 74–83.

Opp, G. (1994). Historical roots of the field of learning disabilities: Some nineteenth-century German contributions. *Journal of Learning Disabilities,* 27 (1) 10–19.

Orton, S. T. (1925). "Word-blindness" in school children. *Archives of Neurology and Psychiatry,* 14, 581-615.

Orton, S. T. (1937). *Reading, writing and speech problems in children.* New York: Norton.

Payne, N. (1993). [Learning disabilities in the workplace]. Unpublished raw data.

Pollan, C., & Williams, D. (1992). [Learning disabilities in adolescent and young adult school dropouts]. Unpublished raw data.

Rawson, M. B. (1988). *The many faces of dyslexia.* Baltimore: The Orton Dyslexia Society.

Steeves, J. (1987, November). *Computers: Powerful tools for dyslexic children.* Symposium conducted by the Orton Dyslexia Society, San Francisco.

Stricht, T. G. (1987). Functional context education. In *Workshop Resource Notebook.* San Diego: Cognitive Science.

Tallal, P., Miller, S., & Fitch R. (1993). Neurobiological basis of speech: A case for the pre-eminence of temporal processing. In *Annals of New York Academy of Sciences,* 682 (6) 74–81.

Taylor, S. E. (1960). *Eye-movement photography with the reading eye.* Huntington, NY: Educational Developmental Laboratories, Inc.

U.S. Department of Labor. (September, 1992). *The literacy needs of job seekers served by the U.S. department of labor.* Princeton, NJ: Educational Testing Service.

Weisel, L. P. (1992). *POWERPath to adult basic learning.* Columbus, OH: The TLP Group.

Weiss, G. & Hechtman, L. T. (1994). *Hyperactive children grown up* (2nd ed.). New York: Guilford.

Wernicke, C. (1874). *Die aphasische symptomencomplex.* Breslau, Germany: Taschen.

Wood, F. (1991, February 25). *Brain imaging, learning disabilities.* Paper presented at the Learning Disabilities Association National Conference, Chicago.

Zametkin, A. J., Nordahl, T. E., Gross, M., King, A. C., Semple, W. E., Rumsey, J., Hamburger, S., & Cohen, R. M. (1990). Cerebral glucose metabolism in adults with hyperactivity of childhood onset. *New England Journal of Medicine*, 323, 1361–1367.

INDEX